Go

Charles Matthews

TEACH YOURSELF BOOKS

For UK orders: please contact Bookpoint Ltd, 39 Milton Park, Abingdon, Oxon OX14 4TD. Telephone: (44) 01235 400414, Fax: (44) 01235 400454. Lines are open from 9.00 - 6.00, Monday to Saturday, with a 24 hour message answering service. Email address: orders@bookpoint.co.uk

For U.S.A. & Canada orders: please contact NTC/Contemporary Publishing, 4255 West Touhy Avenue, Lincolnwood, Illinois 60646-1975, U.S.A.. Telephone: (847) 679 5500, Fax: (847) 679 2494.

Long renowned as the authoritative source for self-guided learning – with more than 30 million copies sold worldwide – the *Teach Yourself* series includes over 200 titles in the fields of languages, crafts, hobbies, business and education.

A catalogue record for this title is available from The British Library

Library of Congress Catalog Card Number: On file

First published in UK 1999 by Hodder Headline Plc, 338 Euston Road, London NW1 3BH.

First published in US 1999 by NTC/Contemporary Publishing, 4255 West Touhy Avenue, Lincolnwood (Chicago), Illinois 60646–1975 U.S.A.

The 'Teach Yourself' name and logo are registered trade marks of Hodder & Stoughton Ltd.

Copyright © 1999 Charles Matthews

Cover photo by Colin Taylor Productions.

Typeset by Charles Matthews.

Printed in Great Britain for Hodder & Stoughton Educational, a division of Hodder Headline Plc, 338 Euston Road, London NW1 3BH by Cox & Wyman Ltd, Reading, Berkshire.

Impression number   10 9 8 7 6 5 4 3 2
Year   2004 2003 2002 2001 2000 1999

Dedication

This book is dedicated to my mother
and the memory of my father.

ACKNOWLEDGEMENTS

This book is my own, but much of the material in it has arisen in the community of Cambridge and British Go players. My thanks are due to Tony Atkins, Adam Atkinson, William Brooks, John Fairbairn, Simon Goss, Andrew Grant, Demis Hassabis, Tim Hunt, Seong-June Kim, Geoffrey Kirkness, Matthew Macfadyen, Patrick Ribbands, John Rickard, Alex Rix, Robert Salkeld, Alex Selby, Edmund Shaw, Paul Smith, Mark Wainwright, Nick Wedd and many others for their contributions. I must thank the British Go Association and in particular Tony Atkins, Gerry Mills, Alex Rix and Francis Roads for their backing. Special thanks, too, to Bill Hartston.

My children George and Heley were concerned mainly that they didn't warrant a mention on the cover, so this is for them from a somewhat absent father. My debt to my wife Clare is harder to discharge. Suffice it to say that she was a brick throughout.

Charles Matthews   Cambridge, January 1999

CONTENTS

1 | FIVE LESSONS FOR THE BEGINNER

A Go player will finish the game before attending a dying parent.

Proverb

Go is one of the most ancient, deeply studied and fascinating of games for two players. Other names for it can be found in the Glossary.

1.1 Go is a game of territory

Go is a game of skill for two players, played on a square grid of lines with round black and white pieces. The pieces are traditionally called 'stones', whether made of plastic, glass, or slate and shell in high quality sets. The standard board size is 19x19 lines, with some markings that don't affect play. Smaller sizes of board are used with the same rules for various reasons: for teaching, to illustrate the game with cut-down examples, and just for shorter games.

The play of the game is simple. One player has a supply of black stones in a container (traditionally a wooden bowl), the other a supply of white stones. Each player, in turn, places a single stone on the board on an empty intersection, called a 'point'. Theoretically there should be 181 black and 180 white stones, but 150 of each ought to be enough. We shall call the players 'Black' and 'White' from now on, and use the capitals for the stones too.

The most important things to point out at the outset are:

- The board is empty when the game starts, except for those games in which handicaps are given.
- The stones are never moved on the board.
- The object of a game of Go is to surround territory on the board.

Go players do talk about 'moves' by Black and White, even though nothing is moved. Stones may be captured and taken off, and then kept for scoring. In the East a game of Go is compared to two armies, settling an unpopulated land. Capture is a secondary object in Go. The main idea is to win by controlling more than half the board. Your aim is to end up in possession of at least 51 per cent of it, not to wipe out the opponent. The chance to capture and the possibility of being captured are important. It is no fun at all playing and being captured everywhere. Capture of stones is discussed in 1.2.

To surround territory you must use your stones to build walls. Edge and corner points count just as much as other points.

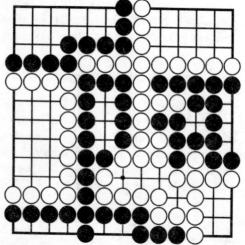

Here is an example, on a 13x13 board, of a position at the end of a game. Black has 15 empty points surrounded in the top left corner, and a total of 13 in other places on the board. Black's total is 28. White has 15 on the left side, 15 in the top right corner, and 10 in the lower right, for a total of 40. White would win this game by 12 points. White has walled off territory much more efficiently than Black, and is a deserving winner. The end of a game comes by agreement. We explain this in greater depth later on. Black always starts in a game of Go. Here Black, having played last too, has one more stone on the board, making 51 to White's 50.

Go players will object that this example is too tidy: the walls are too straight, nothing has been captured, and so on. Patience!

1.2 Capturing stones

A single stone is captured when it is surrounded along the lines.

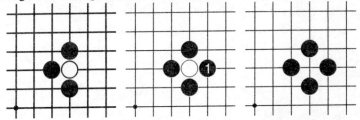

The White stone is captured when Black plays 1, and is taken off the board. The resulting position is shown in the right-hand diagram.

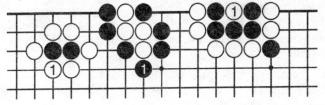

On the edge, or right in the corner, fewer plays are required to capture. The edge of the board is a danger zone.

Several stones of the same colour that are joined together along the lines are *solidly connected*. They must be captured together, if at all.

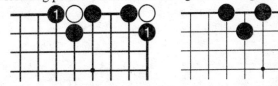

Left to right: White captures two Black stones; Black captures four White stones; White captures five Black stones by a play 'inside'.

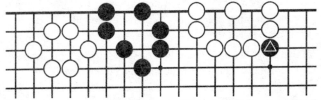

The resulting positions are shown above. Note that the marked Black stone remains.

The Black stone, marked with a triangle, wasn't solidly connected (along the lines of the board) to the five captured pieces. A very common problem in understanding the rules for capture, when first learning to play, is to miss this kind of point about connection. Here are two more examples.

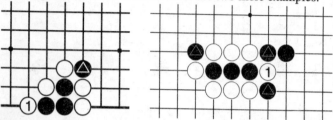

(Left) The Black stone marked with the triangle doesn't prevent White from capturing three Black stones with 1. **(Right)** White can capture three Black stones with 1, none of the three marked Black stones being connected to them along the lines.

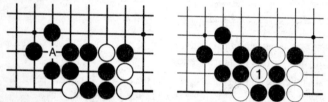

A second important point is that *playing into a surrounded position is allowed*, but only *in the process of completing a capture*. For example in this formation White is able to capture three Black stones by playing at 1. But a White play at A is illegal.

The rules impose no limit on the total size of a capture. There are occasions on which captures of two or more separate 'chains' are made with the play of a single stone. There are some further rules of Go, restricting slightly the legal plays and captures. We shall discuss them in 2.1.

Captured stones are kept by the board in full view, traditionally in the lids of the bowls containing the stones. They are needed for scoring. Each captive is worth one point.

If you are that way inclined, you might be wondering at this moment about the rules of capture, which have been introduced informally. A test of their internal logic would be: are they amenable to computerization? This point is covered briefly in 14.7. It is a simple aspect of what is a hard area, Go programming.

In the complication of a real game position it is not always so easy to see threats to capture. Here is a page of problems.

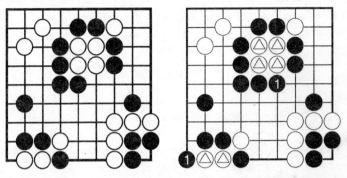

(Left) Which White stones can Black capture? Which Black stones can White capture?

(Right) Black can capture two marked White stones in the lower left, or alternatively four in the centre.

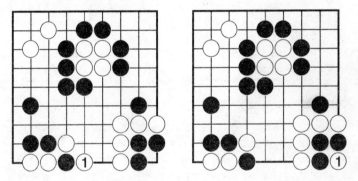

(Left) White can capture one Black stone on the lower edge. This prevents Black from capturing the two White stones in the lower left.

(Right) White can capture three Black stones in the lower right.

The first of these captures achieves something, saving two White stones. The second capture, in the lower right, achieves little. There was no possibility of escape for the three captured Black stones. One of the first lessons to learn is that a capture is in some circumstances a waste of a play. Taking trapped stones may be as pointless as struggling to save them.

1.3 How a game goes

The concepts of 'territory' and 'capture' introduced so far are enough to give a working idea of a game. To recap and add some detail:

1   The board starts off empty in a game of Go.

2   The two players – Black and White – take turns to put a single stone of their own colour on an empty point of the board. Black always starts. A player may say 'pass' instead of playing a stone.

3   The players may play on any empty point, with two exceptions to be mentioned (section 2.1).

4   Stones are captured as shown in 1.2, and are retained by the side of the board, in full view, for scoring.

5   The game continues until both players agree it is finished, by saying 'pass' in succession.

6   The game is then counted. A player's score is the number of points of territory surrounded, by groups of that colour, plus the number of captives taken of the other colour. The player with the higher score wins. A draw is therefore possible when the scores are the same.

While there is more to be said, this summary gives a fair idea of how a game of Go proceeds.

Reading Go diagrams

This book follows Go books in general by using diagrams of the board, or parts of the board, to display positions visually. A point may be referred to by the number of a stone played on it, a mark such as a triangle on a stone, or a letter. This is the traditional system, and makes for easy reading. Where stones are played back on points cleared by the capture of stones, we always note this in the text.

You will probably find it helpful to set up on a board any diagram that isn't very simple. Put on the stones without numbers first, and then add the numbered stones one by one.

The two common systems of algebraic notation are discussed in 14.8, as file formats. They are not much used now in books.

This little game is played out on a 5x5 board. It features a single capture: with the play 12, White captures the Black stone played at 5. Later on White plays back on the vacant point with 16, in response to Black 15, which threatened the stone played as 10. Black 17, too, is a play to save a stone, Black's play 9.

After 17 both players should pass, saying 'pass' out loud. Black has five points of secure territory on the left. White has four points secure territory on the right, plus one captive, total five too. The game is a draw. If White were to play in the territory Black has made on the left, there would be no prospect of the White stone surviving. Let's look at this point.

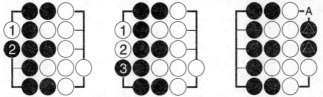

The left-hand diagram shows how a White invasion fails – White cannot escape capture after Black plays 2. In fact (**centre**) White has no chance if allowed two moves in a row. White's area on the right is even more secure. No Black play there requires White to answer. Even after two more plays (**right**) with the marked stones, Black wouldn't in fact be able to play at A or the lower right corner (playing into a captured position).

The conclusion is that both players are correct to pass after Black 17.

If you don't have Go equipment, you can improvise. Pieces from other games, coins, sweets, washers, wooden pegs in holes, will all do, just to get you started. Many of my first games were played with pencil and paper, in a squared exercise book. Some use a whiteboard or computer screen. I'll assume you can follow me as we go. Supplier information for mail order is given in 14.10; or try a good games shop.

1.4 The principle of two eyes

There is a single tactical principle that dominates thinking about what is happening on the Go board. It isn't even really possible to explain how the game ends, without mentioning the 'principle of two eyes', and justifying it. It isn't a rule, but a practical consequence of the rules about capture. It was seen in action in 1.3, in the discussion about the end of the game.

You can understand why these Black stones may be taken by White.

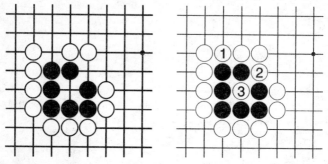

White can play 1 and 2 here in either order. Going back to what was said on p.4 about capture, by playing into a surrounded position, the play 3 must come last of all.

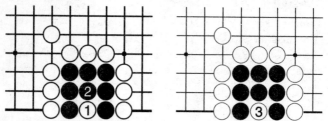

Again, in this case, White has to play inside last of all. White 1 is captured by Black 2, but White 3 recaptures, taking all eight Black stones.

These two examples are of groups with a single eye. 'Eye' means a properly defended space inside the group: one that never need be filled in.

According to the 'principle of two eyes', *a group with two eyes is safe from capture*. You may find this easier to understand in a few concrete examples, such as the four given on the next page. There is an important converse (see p.14). For the present we say: *if a group hasn't got two eyes, and has no way of making them, that group is in serious danger of eventual capture.*

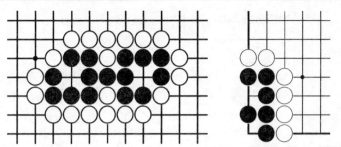

These are examples of groups with two eyes. White can make no progress in trying to take them. White plays in the eyes would be into captured positions (they are even illegal, 2.1). White has to admit these groups are safe, unless Black fills in one of the eyes by mistake.

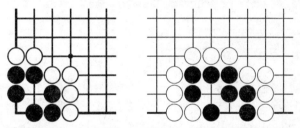

Here are two more groups with two clear eyes. The Black stones in them are not fully connected up, but are safe collectively – this justifies the use of the word 'group'.

Beginners often waste plays making well-defined eyes, or three or even more eyes. You need the *potential to make two eyes*. If you are able to make two eyes whatever the other player tries, you are safe. This is often found hard to understand, to begin with.

Problems

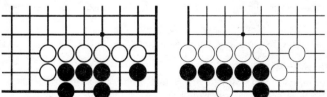

How can Black ensure two eyes in these two groups? Black to play and survive! Problems of this sort, called 'life and death', have been composed in large numbers. They range from easy, such as these, to fiendish.

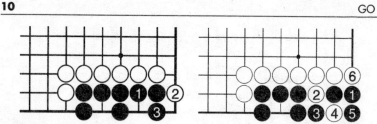

(**Left**) This shows the correct way to play in the first problem. Black can form a second eye with 1 and 3. There is trouble ahead if Black tries a different method (**right**). With 1, 3 and the capture 5 Black doesn't form a genuine eye. It is a so-called 'false eye': a space inside all right, but not properly defended. When White plays 6 there is a threat to the three Black stones, and Black will not benefit by efforts to save them (if Black connects by playing at 4 White can threaten the whole Black group).

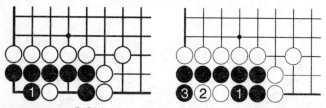

The correct answer (**left**) in the second problem leaves White with no way to attack. One of Black's eyes has a White stone in it, but is none the worse for that. The wrong answer (**right**) leads nowhere. Black can capture White with 3.

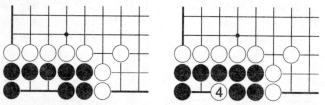

But (**left**) this is like the second example on p.8. When White plays inside once more (**right**), it is clear that Black cannot survive.

In a game, both Black 3 and White 4 in these diagrams would be mistakes, wasting plays. The capture with Black 3 doesn't save the Black stones. The White play at 4 isn't required to stop Black making two eyes.

The first answer depended on a basic principle: *widen the eye space*. The second problem illustrates the other major principle: *partition the eye space you have*.

1.5 About the end of the game

Experience shows that it is the end of a game of Go that causes the beginner most trouble. It is all very well to say that under Rule 5 of 1.3 it goes on until the players agree it is over. They can do that by each saying 'pass'. But what exactly have they then agreed to? Both players see clearly which stones are able to form two eyes and so are safe, and which are hopeless; and that all territories are safe from invasion. If not, they play on.

Here is a 7x7 game with some extra plays at the end. It also has a sting in the tail. There is an honest difficulty about the end.

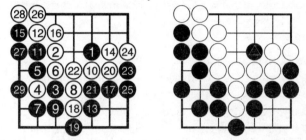

(**Left**) A single piece (White 4) is captured. Black 27 is the final play with real value. What happens then?

The White play 28 is a *neutral point*. It doesn't affect territory. The capture at 29 is necessary after 28, to save four stones. Both players should say 'pass' at this point. At the end of the game (**right**) the marked Black piece is hopeless, with no prospect of two eyes. It is removed from the board at the end – by passing, Black agrees to this.

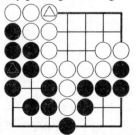 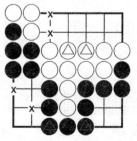

Two further steps are always taken.

    ■ (**Left**) The captives are placed inside the territory of the owner.

    ■ (**Right**) Stones are moved from the 'x' points to ease counting.

This is a draw once more, with 10 points each. In fact drawn games are not so frequent in practice.

The plays on the board settle various issues to do with territory and capture. When the players pass, they are using a protocol saying that all the issues have been brought to a definite, agreed conclusion. It happens that this game really was over when White 26 was answered by Black 27 – full details are on p.134. *This isn't meant to be obvious.* If both players were quite strong the game would indeed have the agreed end shown. If not, the issue of the hopeless stone at Black 1 might have been decided another way, before the players passed. If White had played inside the top right corner to suppress it, that would have lost a point of territory, and the game.

Reading on

You can read on in this book in several ways.

- ■ If you feel you would like to have some further general ideas about Go to work with, try Chapter 2.

You can come back to these extra lessons whenever you like.

- ■ If you would like to move on immediately to the basic tactics of Go, read sections 3.1 to 3.9, 4.1 to 4.4, and 5.1 to 5.7.
- ■ If you would like to see some real games of Go, look at Chapter 6 or Chapter 13 without worrying too much about the comments.

To follow the games you should read the rule of *ko* in 2.1 now.

- ■ If you like the idea of studying Go strategy, you can read Chapter 9 at an early stage.
- ■ If you like puzzles, try setting up problems from the later chapters on a board, examining them for five minutes, and then looking at the solutions.

Start playing Go on a 9x9 board. Without some overall idea of how to play, you may find a 19x19 board baffling. If you are a natural games player, you can reject this advice; not all Go teachers agree with it. Go relies on intuitions that build up gradually. Try to find opponents, in a club, online, or in the form of a computer program, who will play small board games against you as you find your way into the game.

2 | FIVE FURTHER LESSONS

2.1 Further rules: *ko*, suicide, *seki*

There is a simple kind of situation, occurring in most games of Go, which could lead to a repetition of position if nothing were said otherwise.

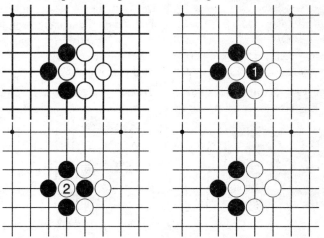

In this sort of position, Black could capture one White stone with 1, and then White one Black stone with 2. The final position would be the same as the initial one. To combat this there is the

Rule of *ko*: In a position where one stone has just been captured (in the centre as shown, on the edge or in the corner), the player with the turn may not take back to leave the same position.

But this prohibition lasts for one turn only. If it matters who gets control of the intersections being disputed in the *ko* situation, the second player may use a threat that has to be answered, elsewhere on the board, to buy time to recapture. Then the boot is on the other foot. Long sequences of such *ko* threats and *ko* captures may occur, leading to exciting, difficult and (unless you are a very good player) unpredictable exchanges and consequences. There is much more said in Chapter 7 about the effect this rule has on the game.

The second of the two rules forbidding a play on an empty point is the

Rule of suicide: You are not allowed to play suicide moves.

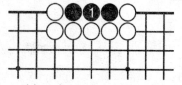

For example, in the position shown here, Black 1 would lead to all three Black stones being captured at once. This is an illegal play. For the most part suicide plays wouldn't be useful, but you might actually want to use this one as a *ko* threat against White's eyes. *Playing into a captured position while completing a capture is legal,* as was mentioned in 1.2. With what was just said about *ko* this completes the explanation of Rule 3 of 1.3.

There is another rule about which the beginner should be warned, though it is less likely to come up in your first few games.

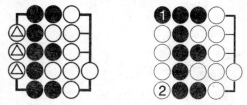

This position could have been shown in 1.3. If Black unwisely allows White to play three times inside the territory on the left, without answering, we may get the diagram shown (**left**). The White stones with the triangles are now safe from capture. Black tries (**right**) but is taken. White equally cannot capture Black. The left diagram is an example of the situation known as *seki*. Neither player wishes to continue to play in this part of the board.

Rule of *seki*: Neither player counts any territory in a *seki* position.

Therefore if a *seki* position persists until the end of the game, the area involved is simply left out of counting, and isn't rearranged in any way. Your stones in it survive but you score nothing there. The correct way to state a converse of the 'principle of two eyes' of 1.4 is that *a group that is unable to form two eyes will die, or end up in a* seki *position.* This rule is explored more deeply in Chapter 7.

2.2 How to compete

The concepts and rules given so far are more than enough for you to play your first few games of Go. You need some experience to digest them.

One very direct way to gain access to Go tactics is to try 'capture Go'. Make the object of the game simply to be the first to take one of the opponent's stones; then to be the first to take three; then five. This cut-down version of Go is most suitable for two complete beginners, who will quickly pick up on threats to capture.

Soon you'll need guidance on how to conduct a whole game of Go. The object of this section is to give enough pointers to lift your game onto the next stage, beyond making direct threats.

Defend your territory

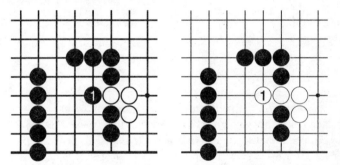

Sometimes the most important play on the board will be simply to defend a territory that is almost complete (**left**). In this position Black would make little territory with the walls shown if White were allowed to play at the point of Black 1 (**right**).

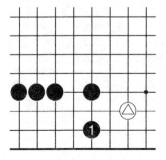

Black protects territory to the left. White would happily slide to the point of 1 from the marked stone, reducing Black's area. It is important not to allow one's opponent simply to push into territory.

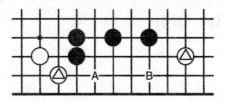

An area of the board like this is hard for Black to make territory in, since White can come in on either side at A or B, backed up by the marked stones. With an 'open skirt' on either side, the advice is: Black shouldn't expect to make much territory here.

Keep connected

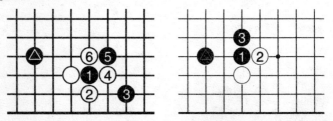

The games of novice Go players are full of sequences like the one on the left, with White 6 completing a capture. None of Black 1, 3 and 5 is connected to another; and none of them seems to be played taking account of the original Black stone marked with a triangle. In general it is much better to build up your formations as shown in the right-hand diagram. Here, Black 1 is played in relation to the triangle stone, so that they support each other. And then Black 3 is solidly connected to Black 1. The resulting position is solid and coherent.

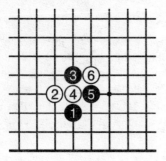

It would probably never occur to a good player to answer White 2 here with Black 3. Trying to jump ahead this way leaves Black very obviously weak after 6. Black 3 would be much better at 4.

Learn to sacrifice

In some Go clubs, the kind of game you might be offered as a complete beginner would be a handicap game on a 9x9 board. The handicap would consist of a number of Black stones placed on the board before White starts. Here Black has been given four stones, one in each corner.

In the game shown Black resolutely sacrifices the top right corner, leaving the stone there to its fate. In return, the wall built with plays 2 up to 12 should make the rest of the board into Black's territory. Black now ought to win easily, with a massive 50 or so points of territory, to about 10 for White in the top right.

Stay ahead in capturing races

A position like this is a race to capture. Whoever plays first wins.

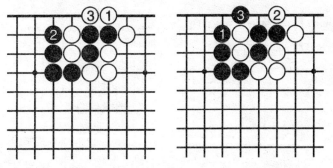

There are many refinements in capturing race tactics. But the first principle must be, pay attention, and stay ahead if you start ahead.

2.3 Wall Street

A Go player need not think greed is good, but the old saying about balancing greed and fear applies remarkably well in Go. You must have a keen appreciation of formations that work well. If you are too fearful, or inefficient, playing your stones too close to each other, you will fall behind. Walls and rectangular territories are the simplest formations, but remarks about them are still illuminating. See also 9.6, 9.7 and 11.7.

Two walls in the corner, three on the side

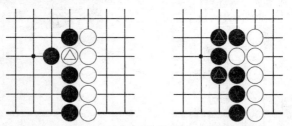

A picture explains quite easily why nine stones make nine points on the side, where only six stones are needed in the corner. On the same basis 12 stones are needed to make four walls and nine points in the centre. You can say that a wall gains greatly in efficiency, by standing in close relation to the edge. It seems plain that plays near the corner may work up to twice as hard in surrounding territory as plays in the centre. This accounts for the great importance of the corners in Go strategy. It is usual to start there.

Straight lines work best

White spoils Black's straight wall (**left**) with the marked stone. It is likely that Black will have to add the two further marked stones (**right**) to avoid tactical problems, making a big loss of efficiency.

Scaffolding and building

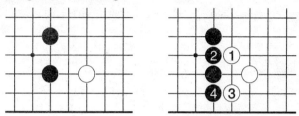

Substantial territories aren't completed all at once, any more than Rome was built in a day. **(Left)** Black seeks efficiency by placing two stones that are not directly connected, and has the makings of a wall. **(Right)** Black is prepared to fill in the gaps if required, when White challenges. Black is at a safer distance from White than in the previous example, so can afford to stretch a little further.

Height of achievement

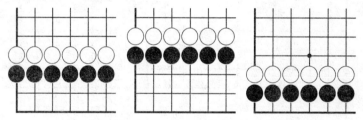

(Left) It is often said that these walls (Black on the third line, White on the fourth, speaking as Go players do and counting in from the edge or first line) are of equal value: that White should earn as much on the outside as Black does on the edge. **(Centre)** Black's wall and the edge territory it gains are better than White's wall. **(Right)** White's wall is better.

These comments are justified for a 19x19 board, but not for smaller boards. Reducing it to a matter of arithmetic: if Black occupies the third line and White the fourth line all round a 19x19 board, check that Black wins 136 to 121 on the territories so defined. But that is with all four corners going to Black, and the effect of White's wall overlapping. It represents, therefore, something of an underestimate of the worth of a fourth line wall. Such calculations are a reasonable tool in assessing strategies on the large scale.

2.4 Handicap games

Go players measure their progress by a system of grades, comparable to those awarded in martial arts such as karate. The difference in grades is used to set handicaps – if players are seven grades apart the weaker player takes Black and a seven stone handicap. The handicap system is discussed at greater length in 14.9. Point handicaps, called *komi*, are also common. Players of the same grade usually now play with White receiving six points *komi*. If they are one grade apart the weaker player takes Black.

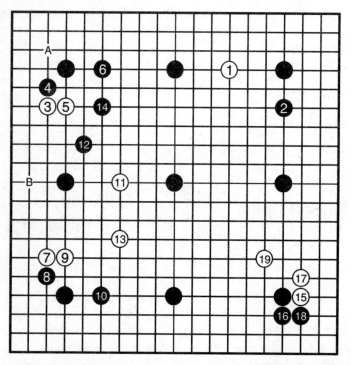

Here is an example of play in a nine-stone game. When you first encounter a *dan* (expert) player, he or she is likely to offer you a nine-stone teaching game. It is polite to accept, whether you think more or fewer stones might be appropriate. If you win, your level is probably around 10 *kyu* (club player). Note that the fewer *kyu* the stronger you are; then, after passing from 1 *kyu* to 1 *dan* (also called *shodan*, or entry-level master) the more *dan* the better.

The advantage conferred by the nine handicap stones, shown placed in position on the small 'star' markings on the board, is very large, perhaps 100 points. If Black feels there is no way to lose, though, Black has another think coming. To illustrate what is going on, let's eavesdrop on White's thought processes – as the expert White can give us some insight.

'Black answers 1 at 2. That's the best play, but I can move on to another area. White 1 won't get into any trouble I can't handle.'

'Black answers 3 at 4. Best move again. Black has played before! I need 5 to avoid getting squashed. Then 3 and 5 are much harder to defend or sacrifice than 1. The handicap stone in the middle of the left side now cramps the style of this group.'

'Black 8. Perhaps Black should just have played at 10. On to 11, a very loose capping play. I get a chance to attack the handicap stone on the left side on the large scale. But basically it's a bluff.'

'Black 12. Right idea. Black has to lead the stone out, or give it up. Making life in place on the left is a bad idea. I was really afraid of this one.

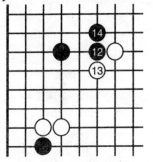

Avoid getting shut in! If on move 12 Black makes this shape recommended on p.16, White's supposed attack on the left-hand side comes to an end. White's stones there would all be vulnerable.

'Not much I can do if Black finds excellent plays like that, though. Black would be safely out in the centre. I'd have problems.'

'White 13. Time for a little defence. This does something to hold me together here, and I can aim to invade the lower left later. Black 14 doesn't finish off the two stones 3 and 5. I can play at A or B to use them later. Just now I'm busy getting round the board.'

'White 15. I get to play in the fourth corner of the board. I'm going to try something a bit more aggressive, to see what Black is made of. Ah, answers at 16 rather than at 18. If Black had gone at 18 I could have played at 16 to complicate the issue. As it is, I really shouldn't push on into the corner. A diagram on the next page shows why.'

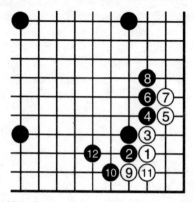

'This (from 1 to 12) is the normal sequence when White invades directly at the 3–3 point behind Black's handicap 4–4 stone. If I go down this road I just make it easy for Black to build in the centre. But I can get landed with exactly the same result if I play 17 at 18, in the diagram on p.20.'

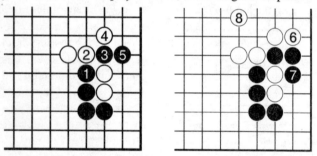

'I like 19 as an idea. I can get cut, sure enough. Then I give up two stones **(left)**. Maybe the honest thing is to carry on **(right)**. But I might leave that for later, moving on to the 3–3 point A in the top left now.'

Rather than follow White's thinking any further, let's summarize:

- Initially White is much more concerned with issues of attack and defence than with territory.
- White aims for speed of development.
- White doesn't get bogged down in trying to capture Black.
- White is happy to sacrifice stones.
- White avoids invasions that serve to solidify Black.

Black should counter by using the 'influence' of the handicap stones (see 11.1). These are all useful ideas for play in even (i.e. non-handicap) games.

2.5 Counting, reading, decisions

Go is enjoyable because it is not just a question of exact calculation and analysis. Intuition has a respected part to play. If you think you can rely on predicting the future course of the game, and don't pay enough attention to apparently vaguer questions such as 'How can I get my stones to work well, to build territory or for attack?', you can't expect to progress quickly.

A highly analytical, structured approach to playing Go might focus on the problem of scale: the 19x19 Go board has a large playing area. It is natural to break it into parts that are considered separately. In a real game it may be hard to see the potential coupling or uncoupling of areas – to make systematic use of the idea that the board falls into smaller areas that interact weakly, if at all. The examples given in this section are three case studies supposed to 'send Go to business school'. Here are the tools:

- ■ **Counting:** Strong players pay great attention to assessing the score as the game is in progress, as a guide to strategy. This is simple in principle: visualize the future boundaries for territories, and count them, in each part of the board. But demanding in practice. Begin by working on your endgame.

- ■ **Reading:** The exact analysis of particular situations. One's reading can be improved by the study of Go problems.

- ■ **Decision-making:** Must take into account the input from the first two but also other factors, such as intuitions, pattern-matching, knowledge of one's own strengths and weaknesses, the need to simplify or complicate the game.

Case 1 By counting alone

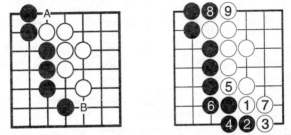

A counting decision. White at B is worth more than White at A. White wins by two points. White at A would lose points and the game to Black at 7.

Case 2 Life in unpromising circumstances

It looks here very much as if the six White stones on the left will have to find safety on their own. The marked White stones on the right are apparently too far away to help. And if that is the case then White will fail to make two eyes and get life for the six stones.

In fact there is an interaction between the two parts of White's position.

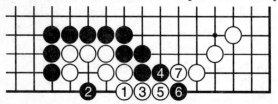

When White plays 1 here, it sets up the chance of a definite connection along the edge, as shown. The triangled White stones are part of a group that has no trouble in making two eyes. White has saved the six stones on the left.

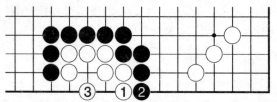

But if Black in some way blocks the escape route along the edge, White makes two eyes with 3. White 1 looks innocuous but in fact counts as a double threat.

What is characteristic of Go as a great game is the way more complex problems arise from the simplest of elements, as here. And not just artificial difficulties, either. Games between players without a great deal of experience, can throw up positions of interest to those who are much stronger. One reason is this sort of tangential possibility or side-effect.

Case 3 A costly intrusion

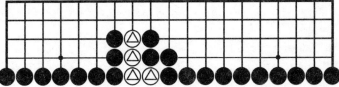

Black seems to have done well here, taking almost all the side. There are some intrusive White pieces. We assume they are part of a two-eyed White group. What effect do they have? This is tricky to quantify.

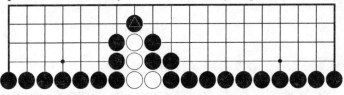

If Black completes the territory like this, it amounts to 68 points.

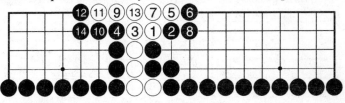

It may look as if White does well playing out this endgame sequence, reducing Black's territory by 13 points to 55 points, and retaining the move. These plays are standard, and are treated in some detail in 8.10.

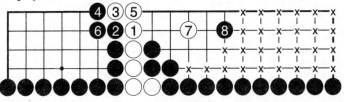

In fact, White has a better way to play, as shown here. See also p.59 for the tactic 7. Black's total territory would be at most 50, even counting all 28 'x' points. This example combines counting (accurate or estimated) with reading (choice of move). The final diagram, with White 1 a double threat to the two Black territories, shows exactly that they are not independent. One should evaluate a play here as worth at least 20, rather than 13 points.

3 | CAPTURE

Now we begin a thorough study of the tactics of Go. Everyone must understand the point of knowing first how to capture, and avoid being captured. Note that the phrases 'captured in a net', 'captured in a ladder' and so on use 'captured' in the sense of trapped, not taken off.

3.1 Talking on the chain level

A Go player looks at the board and quickly sorts it visually into solidly connected *chains*. These are the units in terms of which capture works.

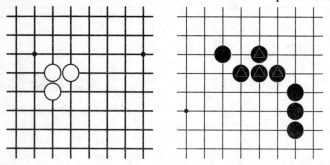

(Left) These three White pieces now form a single unit. For the rest of the game they will stand or fall together. Connecting your pieces solidly is a commitment for the future. If later you find you wish to sacrifice just one of them, you cannot.

(Right) There are three Black chains here. The four marked stones are one chain. The single stone in the upper left is another, the three in the lower right form a third independent chain. The diagonal relation of the isolated stone to the four-stone chain is not a solid connection. If Black later has to give up the single stone, that is possible without involving the others.

What matters in Go is being able to connect solidly, when challenged.

A chain has at least one *liberty,* an adjacent empty intersection. The number of liberties on a chain measures how close it is to being captured. Here are examples of single chains of Black stones with one to four liberties, marked 'L'.

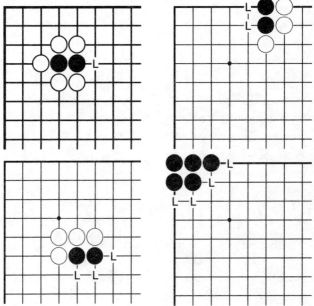

In passing, note how the chains touching the edge in the two right-hand diagrams have fewer liberties than they would if moved to the centre. This effect is even greater right in the corner.

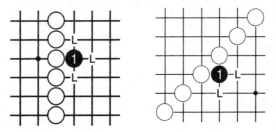

An isolated stone in the centre has four liberties. A play of a stone on its own where it has three (**left**), or just two liberties (**right**), is likely to be poor. Avoid unsupported plays on the edge, too.

The most common problem with understanding capture is to miss the difference between solid connections and diagonal relations. If this distinction still isn't clear, look again at p.26 and the first two examples on p.4. You'll save time later on. The examples given on this page are of White chains (marked with triangles), with from one up to four liberties, in more realistic situations. In each case there is at least one unmarked White stone diagonally related to the chain, but not part of it.

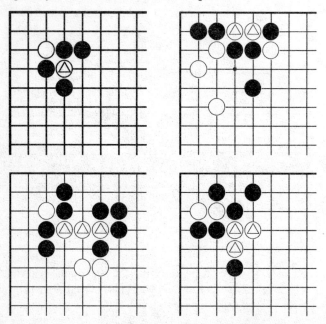

The point to notice is that in each case the White chain with the triangles is a target for Black to capture, independent of the other White stones.

Once the eye is trained to identify the chains on the board, the next step is to recognize those with few liberties, and those with many. Only chains with few liberties are immediate targets for capture by filling liberties. The number of liberties in a chain is a measure of how seriously it is under attack. Fewer than four liberties spells trouble. We shall spend much of the rest of the chapter on cases with two liberties. The set of problems beginning on p.43 goes over a number of the important tactics that apply to capturing chains with three liberties. Chains need five liberties for comparative safety.

3.2 Choosing targets

Aggression works better at a safe distance. Once you are able to see direct threats to your own chains, watch out for the common failing of *playing too close* in the hope of captures.

Here is an attack that fails badly.

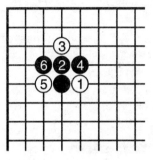

White plays three stones 1, 3, and 5, which end up as three separate chains. Black merely adds to the existing stone to make a single chain, ultimately with five liberties. White is in trouble, with seven liberties spread over three chains. The White stone played as 3 ends up with three liberties, and the others only with two. Look at their positions relative to the Black chain, and compare with the final diagrams on p.27. Black 4 already makes White 1 look as if it was played too close. White is getting nowhere.

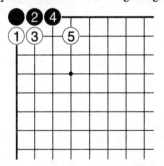

Now for a success story. Whatever Black thought was the purpose of the stone right in the corner, it is an easy target. It will not last long if White goes after it. After White 5 Black cannot save the trapped three-stone chain.

Let's analyse the conditions for White's success here:

- The target Black stone had only two liberties in the first place.
- White chased with 3, adding to the chain formed with 1, not forming a new chain. To play White 3 at 4 is to make the mistake made in the other example.
- White 5 is a clean way of finishing things off. A chase further over to the right might work, or not, depending on encounters with other stones.

This was a simple example of a *net*, about which more later in the chapter. But the three points made are quite general:

- Choose a target with few liberties.
- Don't stretch your own shape just to attack.
- Don't chase on blindly.

3.3 Escape from *atari*

If those points just made are clues to the thinking of the attacker, it should be possible to turn them around for the benefit of the defender. It looks like defence should be along these lines:

- Add liberties to the chain under attack.
- Use weaknesses in the attacker's formation to counterattack.
- Head for friendly forces, given any choice.

Let's apply these first to the case of a chain with a single liberty. It is time for immediate action — the chain may not be there next turn if the opponent captures it. It is 'in *atari*', to use the Japanese term. To 'play *atari*' means to reduce a chain of the opponent's to one last liberty.

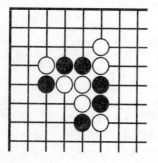

With White to play here, it is the three-stone chain that is down to one last liberty. It is crucial to save it. White has no choice about how to play.

There is no alternative plan in this situation.

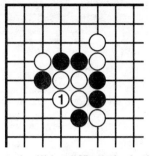

Whatever may come next here, in this truly complicated position, White must start by saving the three-stone chain in the only way available: placing a stone on the liberty to bring the chain up to two liberties.

The sequel will be difficult for both, but that's not the point. If White is captured there is nothing to fight over.

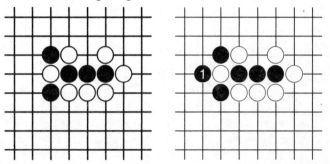

Here Black has a threatened three-stone chain. There is only one way to save it, but this time playing on the liberty doesn't help. The correct thing to do is to capture a White stone (**right**).

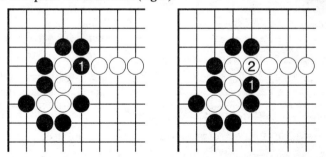

A simple position to show the third way. Black captures (**left**). Black fills the wrong liberty (**right**); White escapes by means of a neighbouring chain.

3.4 Chase down

The more liberties on the chain, the wider the range of capturing tactics that may apply. The rest of the chapter goes over the major possibilities with two liberties. These are the meat-and-potatoes of fighting in Go.

This section covers the first tactical idea one is likely to meet and understand. It is basic: *use the edge of the board to trap stones*. In most games you'll see some single stone on the second line come under threat, at least, of such an attack.

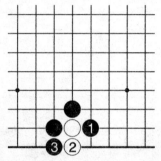

After Black 1 White has no chance of escaping with 2. When Black plays 3 both White stones are clearly doomed. In fact Black 3 isn't even required. You need to be able to recognize this fundamental tactic in many situations.

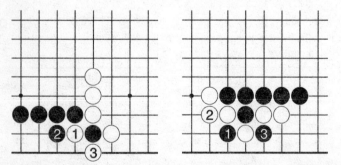

(**Left**) Black gives up the single stone rather than add to it. An endgame play − see 8.10 for more explanation. (**Right**) The chase down can come as the second phase of operations, as in this example. After Black plays *atari* with 1 as shown, White will lose either the stone immediately attacked or the one on the second line.

The chase down idea is certainly not confined to attacks on single stones. It is the number of liberties that matters, not the size of the chain. Here are more examples, including some of the most ordinary errors near the edge of the board. These are very common mistakes in beginners' games.

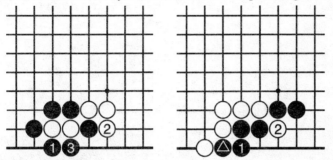

(Left) After Black 1, White cannot save the two stones by playing at 3, and probably plays 2 to limit the damage.

(Right) In trying to save the single stone marked with the triangle, Black is wrong-headed. After White plays 2 four Black stones are lost instead of one.

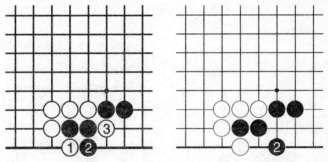

This example is a little different. Black 2 **(left)** is a mistake. You should be able to see why it doesn't now help for Black to take the White stone 1 on the edge. White can continue to attack and soon capture the three-stone chain. Black has lost three stones. Protecting the weakness White exploited at 3 must come first **(right)**, rather than blocking White directly.

Don't worry too much if this sort of disaster happens in your early games of Go. You are in good company! But learn these patterns for the future.

Going back to the case of a single stone, it is wrong to chase it the other way.

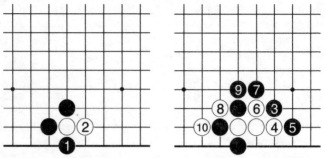

(**Left**) For Black to play this way is wrong in principle. White's two-stone chain started with two liberties, but now has three liberties.

(**Right**) One can imagine Black continuing to attack here. In the continuation shown, White turns the tables. The play 10 captures one Black stone by chasing down, and another one on the edge has become hopeless. White's stones are safe, Black has gained nothing significant. All in all, Black has ignored the good advice in 3.2.

The chase down tactic has a few subtleties, though. We end this section with two examples in which nearby stones matter.

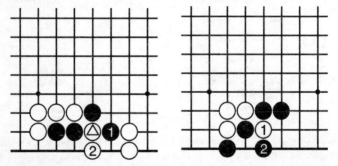

(**Left**) If Black hopes to use it to join up the two chains here, disappointment awaits after White 2. Black has no further attack on the triangle stone because of its neighbours to the right. (**Right**) Black will play as shown, just to be awkward. There is no reason to make the obvious play one point to the left of 2, forming a chain that White can take easily. An unexpected *ko* fight (2.1) is in store in this position. We follow this up on p.109.

3.5 Danger on the edge

One's first few games of Go are quite likely to end with losses of territory because seemingly safe areas are broken into. This has happened to everyone who ever learned the game, just as all learner guitarists suffer from blisters. The most usual cause is a weakness on the second line.

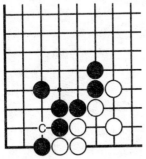

Hardly a game goes by without some formation such as this arising. The point marked C is called a *cutting point*.

Many tactics in Go revolve around such cutting points.

White's plan here makes up in effectiveness what it lacks in finesse.

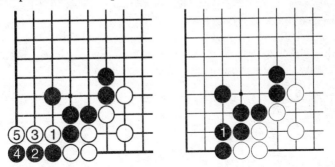

(Left) White 1 captures the Black stone, as the further moves shown demonstrate. Black is chased into the corner. White has only to continue with the obvious plays; White 5 isn't in fact necessary. Black is captured in what could be called a 'one-dimensional ladder', by analogy with 3.7 to come.

(Right) Black ought to defend as shown, to make the corner safe.

Warning! There are many variants on this tactic for breaking in. Cutting points on the second line should be treated with the utmost suspicion. Use great caution in leaving them.

3.6 Double *atari*

After numerous examples of chases using repeated single threats, we come to double threats. Double *atari* means two aims to capture.

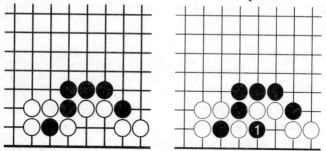

Here there is a two-stone White chain for Black to threaten, in one of two ways. The correct liberty to play on is shown (**right**), because that's double *atari*. Black will now capture one or two stones and break in. Playing *atari* the other way, one point to the right, leads nowhere for Black.

For a change, an odd little example based on breaking out. The old saying from China, 'There are 36 ways to fight, but the best of all is to run away', should be taken to heart by Go players. Almost anything is possible if you can defend skilfully and extricate your pieces from danger.

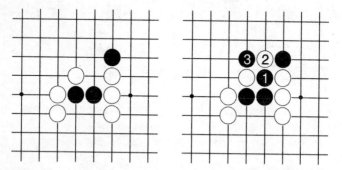

In this case Black can move out in the centre with the two-stone chain. If White blocks the way then Black plays double *atari* and escapes by capturing one or other of the White stones. There is nothing White can do to prevent this.

3.7 Ladders

The ladder is the most spectacular of the capturing tactics (if not as insidious as the *snapback* of 3.9). Ladders can run right across the board. They should not – but we'll come to that in a moment.

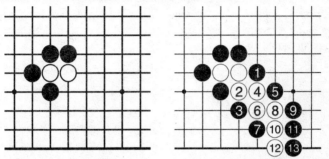

This is the classic ladder tactic. Black's target chain of two has just two liberties. By repeated plays at the 'nose' of the chain, Black manages a chase in which White's liberties never rise above two. With a clear run down to the edge White has no chance. It all ends like a chase down.

What nose means here is the point White requires to make a three-liberty chain. Just as with the chase down tactic of 3.4 Black has to choose the correct way to go each time, or end up in trouble, because the ladder asks the utmost of the attacker's shape. The correct way is to block White's path of advance to three liberties, relentlessly.

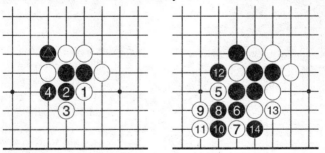

Ladders may fail. A common example is this one or similar. By the time Black plays 4 White will realize that the ladder doesn't work, because of the marked Black stone. Now there is little point persisting – as shown, matters are getting worse by the minute. But White went wrong early on.

What White would find even harder to bear when pointed out is that this was the wrong ladder. There is another one, running south-east, which is perfectly good, and which White could have initiated by playing 1 at 2 instead.

Harder to fathom over the board is the *ladder-breaker*, a distant stone interfering with the roughly diagonal path of the ladder and friendly to the player being chased. One has in practice to figure out exactly what the effect is, or suffer major losses.

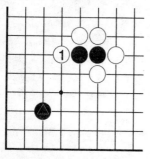 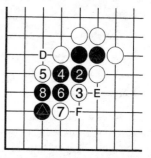

In this example the marked Black corner stone breaks the ladder. If White tries it, Black ends up with three liberties and a pleasant choice of D, E, and F, to make double *atari*.

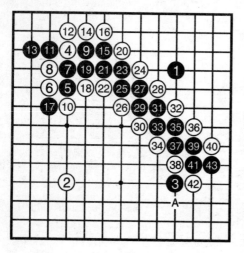

A trap; or, a little knowledge is very dangerous. White 10 is famous as the *small avalanche* play. It depends on a ladder, which is broken by Black 3, (but would not be, by Black A). Disaster for White, who has now to cope with Black's **nine** (count them) possible double *atari* plays.

Ladder lore, ladder lingo

■ With practice ladders can be visualized even if they cross most of the board.

■ It is rare for a ladder to be played out. If it works then the captured side should give up the stones at once; if not it normally does the attacker no good to persist.

■ Playing a ladder-breaker when a ladder capture is already in being tends to complicate the game. Don't overlook the ladder-breaker sneaked in later.

■ So, take off the stones in a long ladder as an urgent priority.

■ It is asking for trouble to set up two crossing ladders at once.

■ One speaks of ladders working, being good, or being unbroken; or of failing, being bad or unfavourable, broken, or not working, and so on, as the case may be.

3.8 Nets on two liberty chains

Another way to capture is by trapping a chain in a net. The picturesque Japanese term *geta*, which actually means a traditional wooden clog, is dropping out of use.

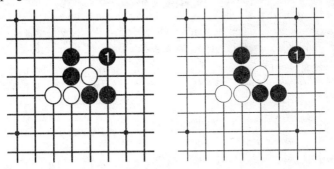

Here are two shapes made by Black that effectively confine a single White stone. You should find it easy to confirm that White cannot escape. (To see the clog, a forerunner of platform soles in Old Japan, you have to look at the Black stones in the left-hand diagram, upside-down.)

The choice often comes up between using a ladder or a net to make a certain capture.

The arguments are not all on one side:

- If the net is possible but the ladder is broken, then use the net.
- If both the net and the ladder are possible, but a ladder-breaker play next would be embarrassing to you, use the net.
- If the ladder works and ladder-breakers aren't a worry, use the ladder to make a stronger shape after the inevitable extra move to take off.

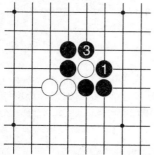

For example, in the same position as before Black might be able to capture in a ladder with 1; and then later will have to play at 3. Compared to the nets shown, Black has a much more solid position, with no weakness for White to exploit, but with one more stone invested.

3.9 Snapbacks

A snapback means a capture of a single stone followed by the immediate recapture of more than one. It is therefore different from a *ko*. In a *ko* the capture of one stone can potentially be followed by the recapture of another. There can be no question in a snapback of immediate repetition of the position.

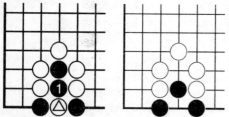

Black 1 captures the marked White stone, White recaptures two Black; then Black can capture one White. But it all stops there.

Experience shows that snapbacks are hard to see coming. They are to be looked out for, at every move. Four classes of snapback formations are given, three in this section and one as Problem 11 on p.45. However, you will still fall into them, as millions have done before. When you find there is less danger of snapback, your feeling for shape will have improved notably.

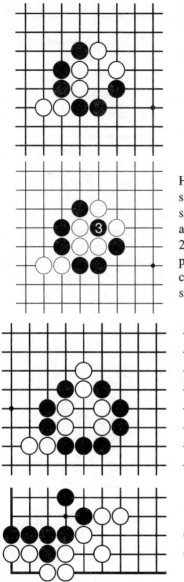

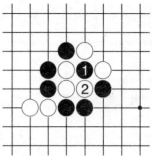

Here are the three steps in a snapback. Initial position; a single stone 1 is played into *atari* and is taken immediately (White 2); Black recaptures with 3, played where 1 was, and taking a chain (of more than one stone, since this is not a *ko* position).

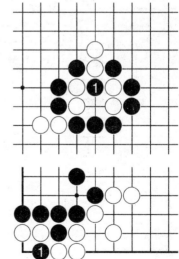

Two more snapbacks, with the play that does the damage.

3.10 Shape lesson – the empty triangle

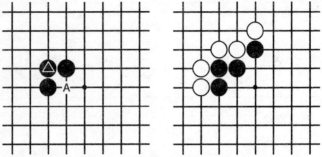

The 'empty triangle' is the shape on the left, with no White stone at A. It is recognized as a bad shape: it (a) is inefficient and (b) lacks liberties. Point (a), the inefficiency of the empty triangle, is seen quite easily. Black can keep the two other stones solidly connected either with A or the marked stone (4.7). When there is a White stone at A, this criticism doesn't apply, since the triangle stone is a useful connection. But the triangle is not empty.

On point (b), three stones in a straight line make a chain with eight liberties; while in the empty triangle formation only seven. All things being equal, one prefers not to be short of liberties. The tactical weakness of the empty triangle is revealed in the position on the right.

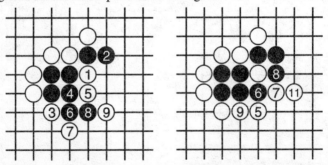

The Black stones may fall victim to a ladder (**left**). Even if that ladder is bad for White, there is still a very good play (**right**) of 'net and squeeze'. Black will have a compact and repulsive shape, an extremely poor use of nine stones. After Black 10 connects, White 11 is excellent. The Japanese use instead of 'squeeze' the word for tie-dying a kimono, and call Black's chain a 'dumpling'.

3.11 Problems

Here are a dozen problems on different aspects of capture. Solutions can be found in 3.12. First, some nets on chains with three liberties.

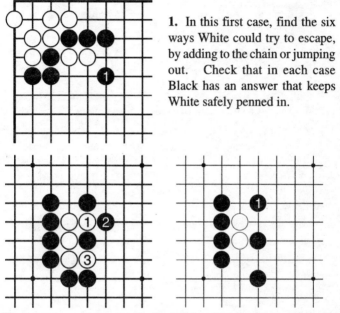

1. In this first case, find the six ways White could try to escape, by adding to the chain or jumping out. Check that in each case Black has an answer that keeps White safely penned in.

2,3. These are two more nets. In the left-hand example show how Black can deal with White's attempt to escape by pushing out, with a sacrifice. In the right-hand example find a ladder involved, and consider what Black should do about it if that ladder is broken.

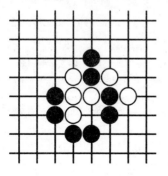

4. A more difficult problem, the *knight's move net*. It is very important for Black to capture the four-stone chain. But how is it to be done? The name relates to the solution. (Players who would otherwise cope easily with the tactics in this chapter very often miss plays like this one, over the board.)

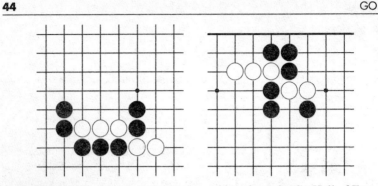

5. (Left) The Crane's Nest. A classic problem from the Go Hall of Fame. What if White tries to jump out to save the three 'eggs'?

6. (Right) Black to play and capture the two-stone White chain. This is a *loose ladder*. The principle is the same as the ladder, but White must be kept down to two liberties with every Black play.

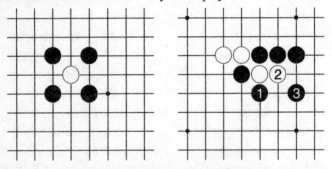

7,8. Bids for freedom. Nets may fail to capture. On the left, can the single White stone escape? On the right, is this really an attempt by Black to net White? How should the game continue from here?

If it is possible to save stones from capture, when is that worthwhile? Which stones may be sacrificed? One of the important Go proverbs runs 'capture the cutting stones'. It means that the most important stones to capture are those that keep your own chains separated. The most important stones to save are those that keep your opponent's chains from connecting.

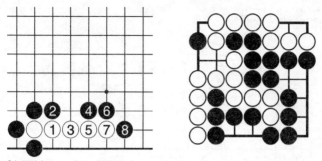

9. (Left) White to play. White has a chain apparently in deep trouble. This position could have arisen in 3.4. Black seems to think that White can be captured by sheer determination. White must find an escape tactic.

10. (Right) Black to play. Should Black pass or play? If Black passes should White pass or play? What would the results be, assuming no captives off the board?

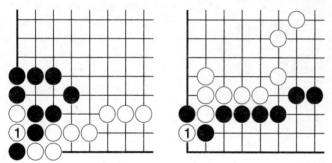

11,12. Why on earth? These plays by White are both sacrifices. But what is their purpose?

After all the emphasis on capture in this chapter, it is good to end with a reminder that taking captives isn't an end in itself. There are many ways of deliberately sacrificing one or a small number of stones to advantage. Knowing when to sacrifice small, to give up hopeless pieces rather than keep adding to them, is fundamental to becoming a good player.

3.12 Solutions

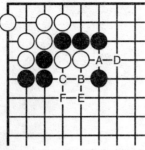 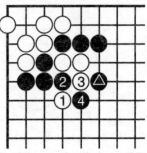

1. The six tries to escape are by A, B, C adding to the chain, and D, E, F jumping out. Black can easily deal with the first three by blocking. The jumps can be cut through. The right-hand diagram shows case F.

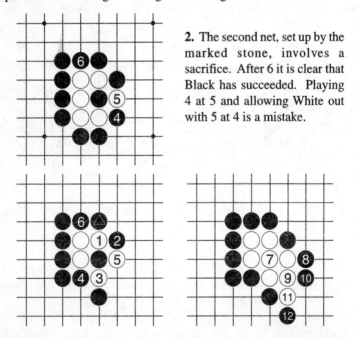

2. The second net, set up by the marked stone, involves a sacrifice. After 6 it is clear that Black has succeeded. Playing 4 at 5 and allowing White out with 5 at 4 is a mistake.

3. The third net really depends on a ladder, as shown in these diagrams. However, even if the ladder is bad for Black, the result will be very poor for White when Black squeezes (**see top left-hand diagram on next page**).

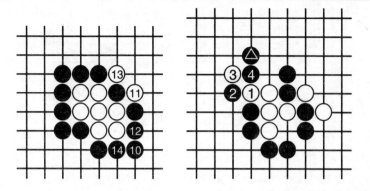

3. (cont.). **4. (Right)** The knight's move net made with the marked stone is correct in this case. **(Below left)** The orthodox netting play fails.

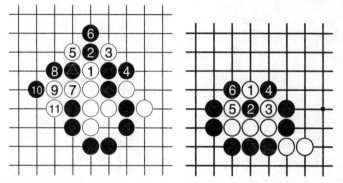

5. (Right) White can't escape the Crane's Nest. The best try is to jump out but when Black sacrifices a piece with 2 and 4 it is all over (cf. Problem 2). Other plays such as White 1 at 2, 3 or 5 fail in more obvious ways.

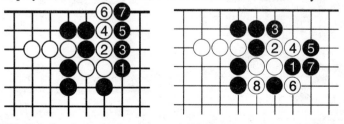

6. This is a simple example, as loose ladders go (see 4.12). Black drives White to the edge and wins **(left)**. It is a mistake to play it like a plain ladder **(right)**. Black 3 is wrong and lets White force a way out.

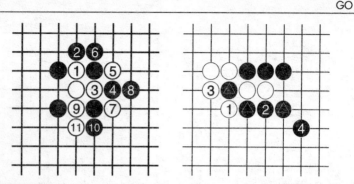

7. (Left) As a matter of Go-playing fact, White can save this piece by pushing out in three directions. It has to be said that this might be much worse in a game than quietly giving it up, at least temporarily, because Black becomes strengthened.

8. (Right) In this case the three marked Black stones don't form a good net. If Black saves the stone in *atari* after 1, White will escape with a play at 2. Black does best to play 2 and 4, making a strong connected group.

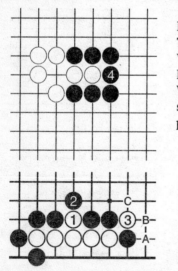

Many players would put 4 here. There is really no reason for White to answer this move. If Black captures two Whites, White can recapture if it ever seems urgent, but these plays are petty.

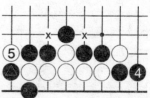

9. Here, White pushes out, and then causes trouble with 3. Black might answer at A, B or C, but White has enough chances to break through. For example **(right)**, with 5 White can capture the marked stone by chase down, or play double *atari* at the points marked 'x'.

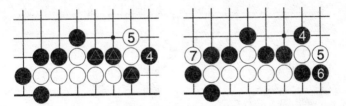

9. (cont.) The other tries for Black. **(Left)** Black will lose at least one of the marked stones. **(Right)** Much the same as Black at A.

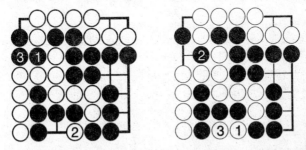

10. Now, no complaints about trick questions, please! You were warned about snapbacks. Certainly neither player should pass. Black to play can kill everything in sight with 1 and 3 **(left)**. Naturally 3 there must not be the capture of 2, which would allow White a snapback. And White to play would capture five Black stones **(right)**.

That word 'shape'

Go players talk a great deal about good shape and bad shape. The shape lessons closing this chapter and the next one only scratch the surface of the subject of shape in Go. But what does it mean?

To play by shape is to use pattern-matching. Few shapes are absolutely right or wrong all the time. But finding some good plays quickly and rejecting some bad plays out of hand is a major help. Go proverbs give much portable wisdom along the lines of 'avoid empty triangles' . Acquiring it should be a major aim for players after playing for a few months.

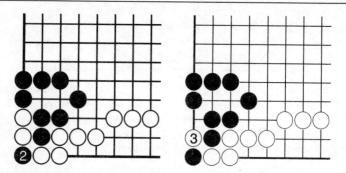

11. This is a (quite rare) fourth type of snapback, associated with the corner. Counting up, White has had two stones captured, and has taken two Black stones. That seems a dull result for the investment of a move. In fact, since Black could make two points by playing where White started, this is a late endgame move, value two.

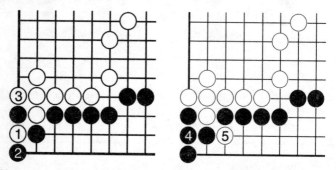

12. The point of White giving up a stone here becomes clear after 3. Black connecting at 4 and allowing 5 — a typical chase down disaster — is out of the question. The sacrifice has stolen a liberty. Black will have in time to defend by connecting at 5, but then White has evidently reduced Black's area by several points for just one stone. There is a chance for Black to fight a niggling *ko* instead (Black at 5, White at 4) but that is a plus for White also.

Summary

The 'chain' concept is useful for a clear understanding of capture. Counting liberties is an important habit to acquire. From now on we move up to the 'group' concept. A group is a collection of chains that support each other.

4 | CUTTING AND CONNECTING

4.1 Groups and connections

Where Chapter 3 explained capture in terms of chains, for the rest of the book we have to recognize that the chain level is the middle layer of structure on the Go board. Below it is the level of individual stones. These are very weak indeed unless co-ordinated with others. And above it is the group level.

- **Individual stones** are very weak. They must be used in combination.
- **Chains** are the right units to consider for capture.
- **Groups** are connected or loose organizations of chains in mutual support.

Groups perform all the interesting functions. Attack, defence, the building of territory and the reduction of the opponent's territories, are all carried out by constructing groups to do the job. Whether they consist of one or several chains is a secondary matter.

It is hard to say precisely what makes a group. The human eye is good at seeing clusters of stones that support each other.

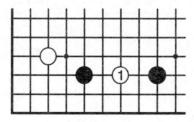

White playing 1 here, seems to divide one Black group into two. That strong intuition needs to be backed up by tactical understanding of connections.

4.2 Cutting points

It is very common for two chains of the same colour to be adjacent to each other, so that they share two liberties.

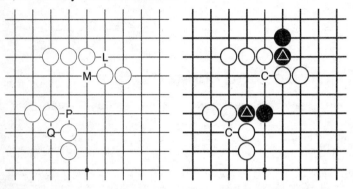

(Left) Two typical cases, liberties L and M, or P and Q, shared, in diagonal relation. **(Right)** The marked Black stone occupies one of those liberties. The other one becomes a cutting point, now indicated by C. We have already met the idea, on p.35. A White play at C would connect solidly.

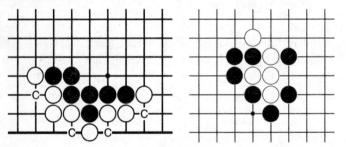

(Left) Four cutting points for White, marked with C. **(Right)** Find three cutting points for Black, and one for White, in this diagram.

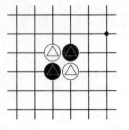

This formation, the *cross-cut*, is important enough to be given a special name. It is the result of Black playing on one of White's cutting points, or the other way round. There are four separate chains here.

4.3 Defended cutting points

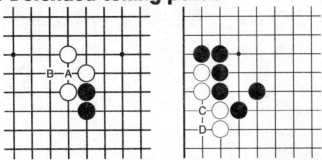

(Left) Here the point A is a cutting point for White, but if Black plays there, White captures immediately with B. This is called a hanging connection, open connection, or tiger's mouth.

(Right) White has a cutting point at C, but if Black plays there White can use a play at D, the chase down tactic of 3.4, to capture.

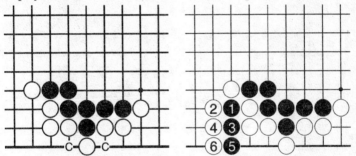

In the example from 4.2, the cutting points marked C here are defended by the edge, and on the left and right sides chase down works.

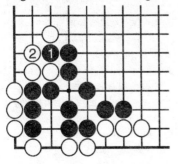

Bridging under. Here White has four cutting points, and Black creates another by playing at 1. But Black has no successful cut.

It is important not to waste time connecting solidly if it isn't necessary to defend further.

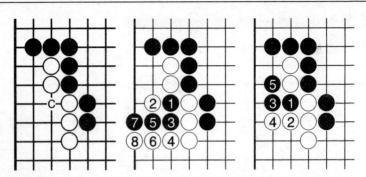

A ladder defends this cutting point for White. The centre diagram shows how White can capture a Black cutting stone. **(Right)** White 2 is a mistake, and White loses two stones.

4.4 Cutting point and *atari* combinations

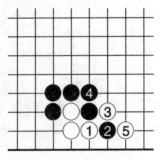

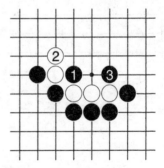

These are common ways to capture stones.

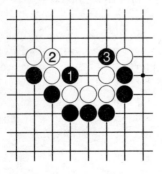

Another example, belonging with the warning about empty triangles (p.42). A typical tactic to break into territory. This pattern of playing 3, with 1 already in place, is surprisingly hard to see coming. I call it the 'shunt'. But I can't say that anyone else does.

4.5 The two-point extension

The two-point extension on the third line is a fundamental part of playing on the sides of the board. ('Two-point' refers to the gap.)

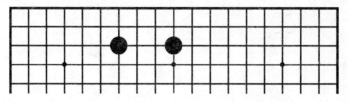

These two stones are close enough to have a secure connection. The diagram on p.51 showed the three-point extension, and how an invasion can separate the stones.

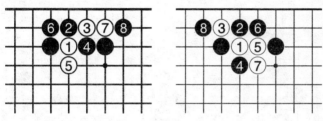

There are a number of ways in which White may try to break the connection. But none of them works. In the right-hand diagram a strong player would choose to play more aggressively with 2 at 4, instead.

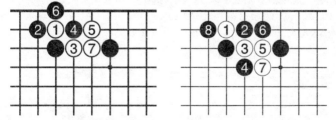

(**Left**) Black has been tricked. This is a bad result. (**Right**) A better way for Black to answer, leading to a result seen before. The Black answer of 2 at 3 is simple and also good.

The two-point extension is the idea most widely used for building a group on the side. It needs further stones to build eye space for two eyes, and may come under attack – but it is a stable way to play.

4.6 The one-point jump, and the wedge

When you want to add to a group in the centre, the one-point jump is the standard play.

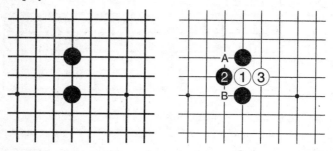

However, it is harder to understand than the case of the two-point extension on the side. The reason is the *wedge* play (**right**) between the stones, leaving Black with two cutting points A and B.

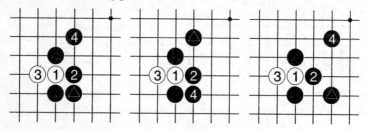

Black can choose on which side to play *atari* against the wedge stone White 1. With one more stone, as here, Black can connect safely. Otherwise it all depends on context. Compare these examples (and also p.101).

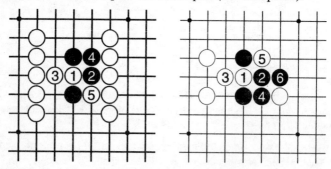

(**Left**) White is very strong, and cuts Black. (**Right**) Unclear result.

4.7 Diagonals and knight's moves

If the one-point jump is too dangerous, the diagonal play is useful.

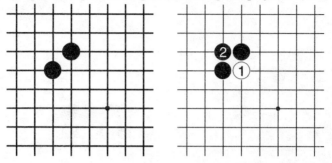

If White plays at one of the points 1 and 2, Black can play at the other one. For that reason there is no immediate way to cut Black.

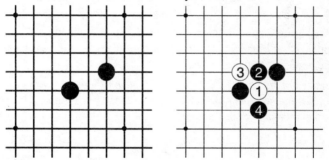

The knight's move reaches further than the diagonal connection. It can be cut, but Black has a good defence if the ladder after 4 works.

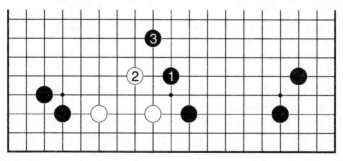

A good use of the knight's move: Black attacks, and starts to form territory.

4.8 Peeping plays

A *peep* in Go terminology means a threat to cut.

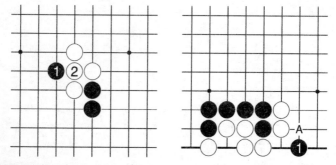

(Left) Black 1 threatens to cut White by playing at 2. Normally White will answer at 2. That leaves an empty triangle, so that the hanging connection isn't always the correct connection as far as efficiency is concerned.

(Right) A peep on the first line. White will feel like playing A first, rather than connecting immediately. It is an empty triangle, true, but this time it may be better than answering passively.

In general it is more often the case that a peep (a threat to cut) should be answered, than an *atari* play (an immediate threat to capture). This shows the importance of keeping connected.

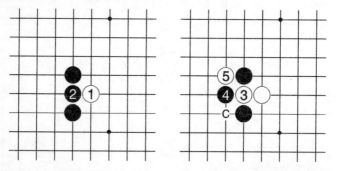

Everyone calls this play by White a peep too, though the threat **(right)** is to push through, then cut at 5 or the other cutting point C. This kind of shape was commented on earlier, when arrived at another way (see p.16). Mostly Black just connects solidly with 2 – but consult the shape lesson at the end of the chapter, too.

4.9 Connecting along the edge

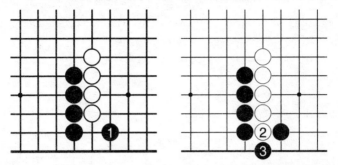

In this position Black can certainly jump as far as 1, to prevent White forming territory to the right. You only have to visualize the right-hand diagram, in which Black's two cutting points are protected by the edge, to see this as an application of 'bridging under', introduced in 4.3.

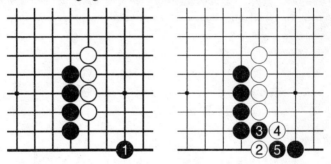

In fact, at times, it would be better to jump like this. Monkeys are indigenous in Japan, and this is known as the *monkey-jump*. White cannot cut it off (**right**), and has to accept a loss of territory.

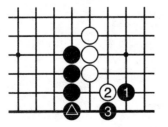

With one more stone in place, the marked one, Black can pull off the 'reverse monkey-jump'. It is a secure connection (**left**), and a skilful play. It was seen in action on p.25. Now it should be easy to grasp.

4.10 The first line, and throw-ins

Cutting points on the first line may seem to be protected, defended as they are by the edge. But they can still cause trouble.

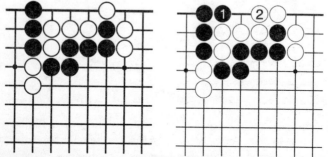

In this position Black would dearly like to capture the four-stone White chain. They are 'cutting stones' dividing Black's forces in two (cf. box on p.44). But the direct approach in the right-hand diagram is a failure.

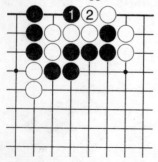

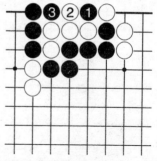

(**Left**) This try by Black is no better. (**Right**) What is required is a leap of imagination to sacrifice one stone. This tactic is called a *throw-in*.

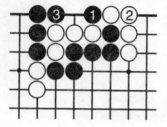

White has another way to answer. But the connection at 2 here is no better. Black 3 captures the cutting stones in a snapback.

4.11 Cutting points on the second line

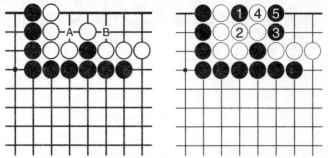

In this case White has two cutting points, A and B. They are both defended. But Black has a very direct way to break into the territory (**right**). Note the order of plays here. If Black starts at 3 then White plays at 1 to form an eye, and wins the capturing race.

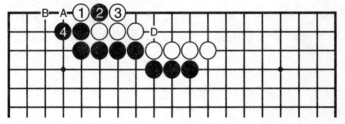

Here's a sharp piece of endgame action. When White plays 1, Black sacrifices a stone with 2. This leaves White with a serious cutting point weakness at D. After White captures and Black calmly plays at 4, White cannot make progress (White A, Black B and White cannot connect at 2 because of Black at D). For the same sort of reason White cannot play 3 at A.

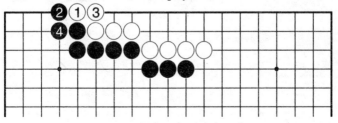

White is one point better off if Black plays this way.

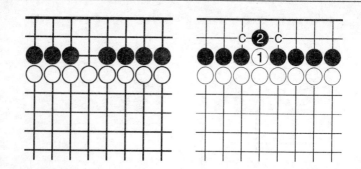

This way of bridging under may work well for Black. The exchange of 1 for 2 sets up two cutting points in Black's territory. But they are both defended (by chase down). Black has one fewer stone here than White, a gain in efficiency. The loss of a point after 1 and 2 is small.

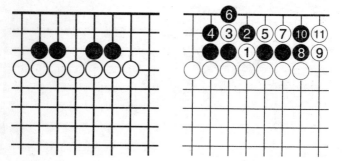

But if Black is noticeably weaker, there may be a serious problem. Two cutting points close together should cause concern. (**Right**) Black must lose some stones.

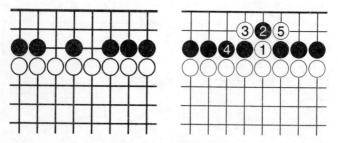

Black is stretched just a little more thinly, White can break through.

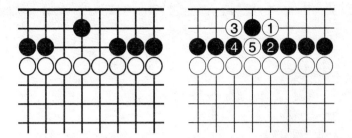

Here the way of breaking through is by cutting right across the knight's moves. This is more sophisticated. Simply creating cutting points with 1 at 2, or 3 at 4, does nothing interesting.

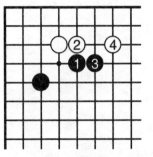 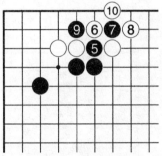

This is a common opening position. What if Black tries the same idea (**right**)? It isn't interesting for White just to play 8 weakly at 9.

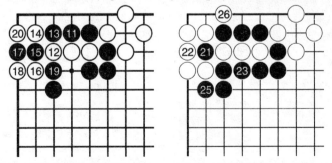

The capturing race is excitingly close (White 24 is played at 21). Black pulls all the stops out with the two-stone edge squeeze from 15 onwards. But White is ahead by one liberty at the end. Can you see how White should answer now if Black plays to the left of 26?

4.12 Weak nets, ladders that are too loose

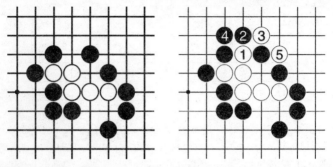

Here White has four liberties, and can easily escape Black's net. What is required is to push out at 1, create some cutting points, and threaten double *atari* with 3. Then White can capture a stone.

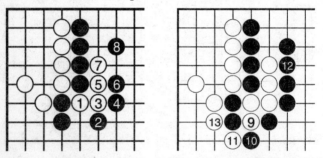

White cuts at a cutting point. If the ladder running south-east is bad for Black, there is this loose ladder to try (see p.44). Black can't capture White in this case, so may settle for the net with 8. White escapes (**right**), but Black's resulting wall is useful.

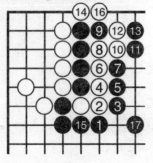

This is the reason that the loose ladder fails in its main variation, in this case. Black has one liberty too few. Other ways to play, such as 5 at 6, and 7 at 8, fail more obviously. Even so, Black's result to 17 isn't bad. Loose ladders are more complex than ladders.

4.13 Escape

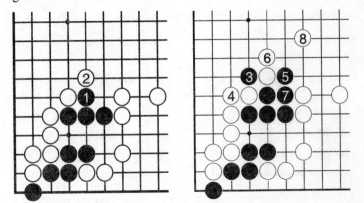

This position shows Black escaping to the centre, by making indirect use of a White cutting point. It is unreasonable for White to cut (**right**) and fall straight into a double *atari*.

Here, pushing to create cutting points isn't enough. Black is netted by the knight's move 8. See problem 13 on p.70 for a variation.

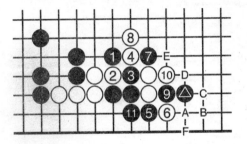

Black escapes to the marked stone after an invasion. White is unable to fight on: after White A, Black B and so on, White loses.

4.14 Skin fights

It can happen that the only way to escape is to cut at some cutting points and capture some stones. 'Skin fight' is my personal term for this sort of position. There was an example in Chapter 3, problem 9.

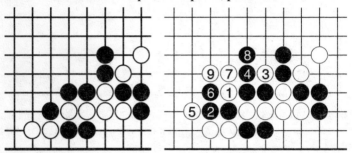

An emergency for White. And a ladder to escape.

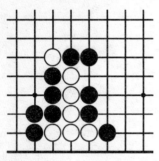
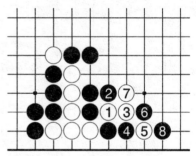

This one is adapted from a quickplay pro game. White to escape.

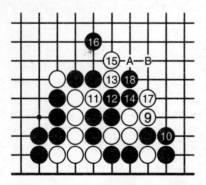

After 18 White has a choice of ladder at A, or net at B, to capture Black. The net is better.

One cutting point on its own may cause trouble. Two or especially three close together are a recipe for disaster. You don't have to be a professional to see that.

4.15 Shape lesson – the bamboo joint

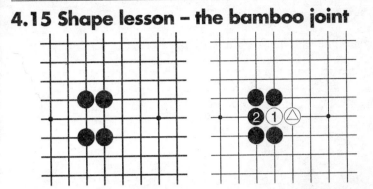

The bamboo joint is the shape on the left. Its most obvious property is shown in the right-hand diagram. The marked White stone doesn't present a threat to cut it – it doesn't work as a peep in the sense of 4.8.

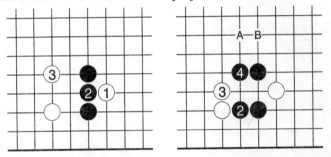

The advantage of the bamboo joint can be seen in a position like this. White peeps against Black's one-point jump (**left**). Black connecting as shown is passive. Playing for the bamboo joint (**right**) leaves Black running out ahead, and able now to jump to A, B, or further.

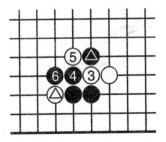

This result is nothing for Black to be afraid of. Both the marked stones are weak. White might choose this way, since 3 in the diagram before doesn't work out well. But it is a fair fight.

4.16 Problems

Fourteen problems, plus a position from one of my games.

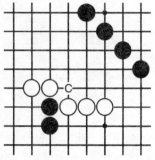 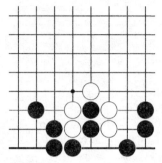

1. (Left) Is White's cutting point C defended?

2. (Right) Black to play and bridge under on the edge.

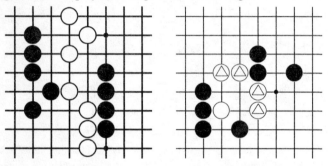

3,4. Black to play and cut White (on the right, cut the two marked pairs apart).

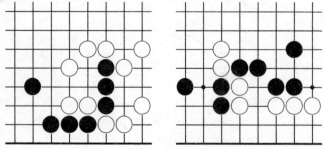

5,6. What one can do with wedges. Both problems Black to play.

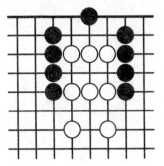
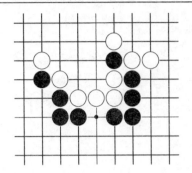

7. (Left) White to play.
8. (Right) Black to play.

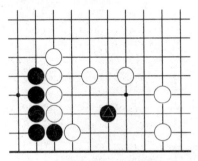

9. Black to play. How does Black rescue the single marked piece in the middle of White's territory?

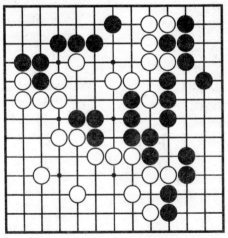

10. Black to play. There is a way to win quickly.

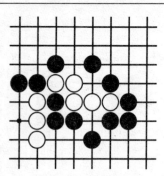
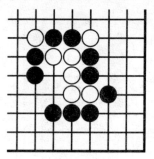

11,12. Can White escape in these two positions?

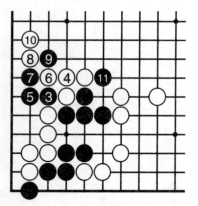

13. This variation could have been shown on p.65. Black is trying very hard to give White trouble. What should White do now?

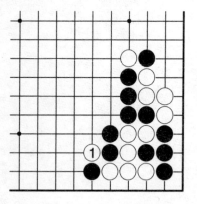

14. Another tricky position in a skin fight. Does White succeed in capturing some stones and escaping?

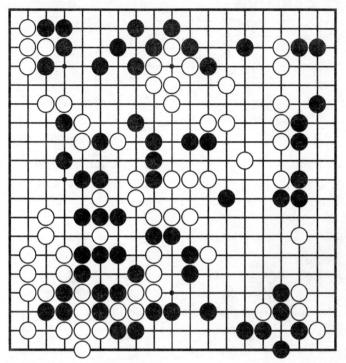

15. This is a position from one of my games from the 1996 British Championship, first stage (Candidates' Tournament). White is behind. But there is still a chance. White to play has to find something special here. Allowing for six points *komi* to White, he is losing by at least 10 points.

The rotten axe

This story is told in several countries of East Asia. A woodcutter comes across two old men playing Go in the forest. Unknown to him, they are Immortals at play. He becomes so engrossed in the game that he loses all sense of the passage of time. When the game finally finishes, it is not only that his beard has reached his toes, the very handle of his axe has rotted away.

4.17 Solutions

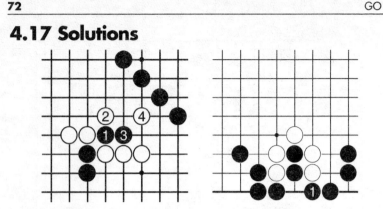

1. (Left) Yes, the cutting point is defended by a net.

2. (Right) Black plays 1, and if White captures the two stones, Black recaptures immediately.

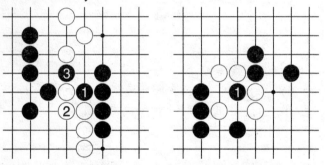

3. (Left) Black 1 is the way to start (3 works too), then Black 2 or 3 according to White's answer. **4. (Right)** Black 1 is the way to separate White.

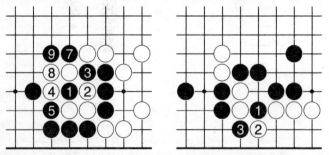

5. (Left) Black captures White stones in a ladder (White 6 at 1).

6. (Right) A snapback. Black captures two White stones.

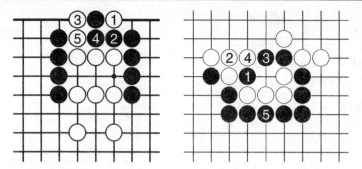

7. (Left) White disconnects Black as shown.

8. (Right) Black gets a snapback.

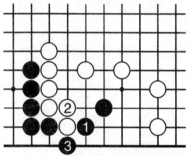

9. After Black plays 1, White will play 2 and Black will connect with 3. If White plays 2 at 3 then Black plays at 2 and captures the White stones.

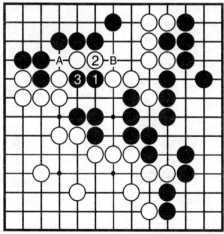

10. This is a case for the bamboo joint. Now Black cuts at A or B.

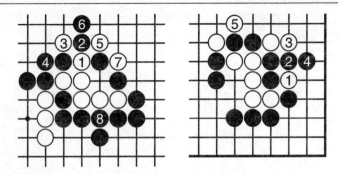

11. (Left) No escape for White. This is a snapback.

12. (Right) It perhaps appears that both ladders are broken. But White makes one of them work, by using the cutting point.

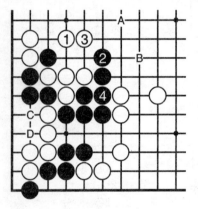

13. It is too dangerous for White to try to keep Black in. White makes sure of the Black cutting stone in a net. Then Black escapes after all. But White is still ahead in the capturing race after Black C, White D. White has captured some stones. And either A or B is a good knight's move attack.

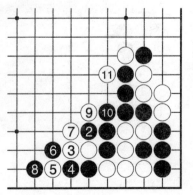

14. White can indeed capture some of Black's stones here. If Black persists then White will be able to capture even more. After White 9, Black 10 leads to the 'shunt' 11.

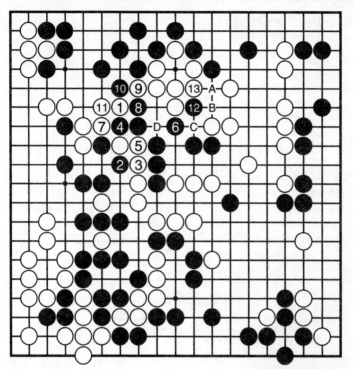

15. This is what happened in the game. There are quite a number of variations, but they all seem to have Black with one cutting point too many, or White with one too few, for the central Black stones to survive. In the final position it may look like a big *ko* fight is to come. But after Black A and White B it isn't a capturing race after all. White will get one of the points C (capture), or D (snapback). Therefore the White stones will live and 10 Black stones in the centre will die.

White gained nearly 30 points with this capture, and went on to win.

Shameful to say, I was White in this game, and my opponent was Simon Goss (2 *dan*), the author of the fine diagram software *gofigs* used in this book.

Summary

Cutting and connecting can be decisive in fighting. If you consistently have too many cutting points to handle, you are probably playing too close.

5 | EYES

5.1 Groups need eyes

Almost all the surviving groups at the end of a game of Go have two eyes, in the sense introduced on p.9 of having the potential to form them. (The other possibility, of life in a *seki*, turns up in perhaps five per cent of games between amateurs.) To have two eyes means that your group isn't vulnerable to attack by an opponent who fills in the space inside.

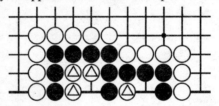

White has spent four plays trying to fill up Black's liberties from inside. However, that was all a waste of time. White has no way to continue the attack. The marked White stones inside are hopeless, and are taken off at the end of the game.

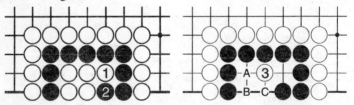

When Black has just one eye, even a big one as here, White can play inside systematically (at A, B, C) and repeatedly, and eventually take Black.

You have to be aware of eyes all through the game. The techniques from this chapter are fundamental. A group containing ten points or more of territory will almost certainly have enough in the way of eye space. Anything less and you should start worrying.

5.2 False eyes

An eye is a defended space inside a group. Every Go player must know
how much defence one point needs to be an eye.

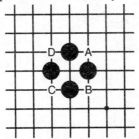

In the centre of the board, the single point surrounded by these four Black
stones may become an eye for Black. Whether that happens depends on
who controls the points A, B, C, and D. Black needs to control three out of
these four points. If White controls two or more, the eye becomes *false*.

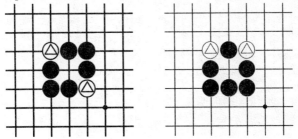

This means there are just two basic patterns of false eye, in the centre. On
the left, the relationship of the White pieces is called *eye-stealing*. On the
right, it is called the *clamp*.

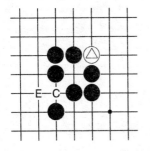

With any three out of four of the
key points, Black is sure of an eye.
In this diagram Black controls the
point C indirectly, through a
hanging connection. That means,
for example, that the play at E
becomes a threat for White, who
could steal the eye by playing next
at C.

The point about false eyes in the centre can be seen by adding more White stones.

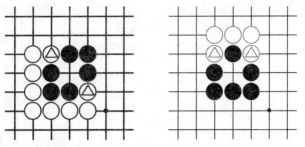

In the left-hand diagram White has added enough stones to put Black's three into *atari*. This means the 'eye' is useless for saving a Black group. In the right-hand diagram the same idea is shown for the clamp.

There is a rare exception to the idea that the eye-stealing relationships destroy the eye (see Appendix, p.212).

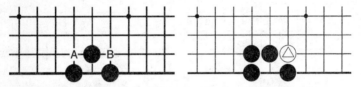

On the edge there is a single, extremely common pattern of false eye. Black needs both points A and B to make an eye. The pattern on the right, in which Black has A and White B, is fundamental.

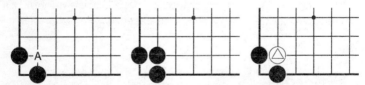

An eye in the corner is the final and simplest case. Black needs A.

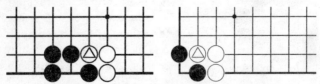

These diagrams show how Black loses the chance of an eye.

5.3 Killing groups by making eyes false

Each of the four patterns of false eye in 5.2 can be put into practice by killing groups – small or large. All you have to do to kill an almost unlimited number of stones is to occupy a key point.

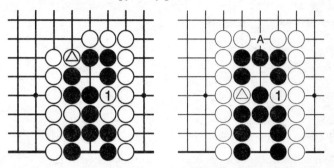

(Left) White's play at 1 sets up the eye-stealing relationship with the marked White stone. It is clear that Black's whole group is dead (i.e. Black cannot prevent its capture). **(Right)** White 1 sets up the clamp relationship with the marked stone. Black is dead. One liberty has been left open at A. If White plays A by mistake, Black plays at 1. Then Black is alive, with two eyes.

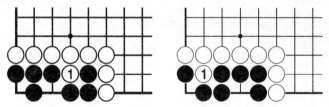

Examples for the edge and corner. More are given in the problems on p.93.

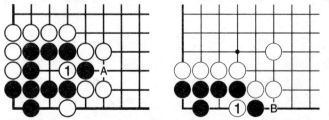

White 1 is a common throw-in technique. Black's eye is false even if the stone is taken. White A or B are wrong – Black plays 1 to live.

5.4 Larger eyes

The eyes shown so far have generally consisted of a single defended point. But there is no reason why eyes can not be formed from larger spaces.

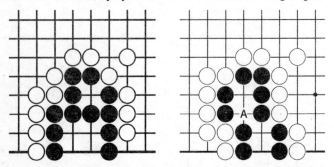

(Left) Here White has the chance to play inside the four-point eye. But as in 5.1 this will be a failure. **(Right)** White can play inside this Black group, for example at A. That is *atari* on two Black stones. But Black can capture the White stone, and still have two eyes.

It is an important point, when one large eye can be divided into two, and is the topic of 5.6.

5.5 Eyes with occupants

If there are stones belonging to your opponent in one of your eyes, that need not be a problem. However, sometimes eyes become false this way.

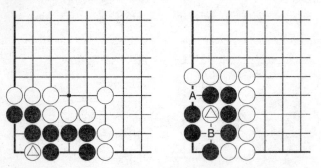

These groups have two eyes. Black answers White A by taking at B.

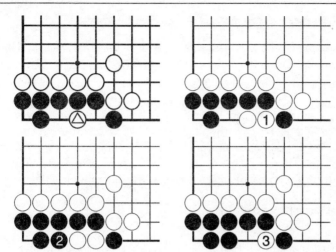

In this example the marked White piece can help make Black's second eye false, as on p.79. Black should play at 1 to prevent this.

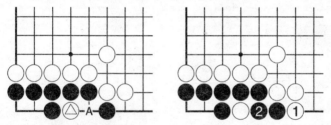

This case is different – Black has two eyes. The presence of the marked White stone prevents White's play at A to make the eye false.

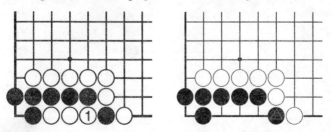

Capturing three stones on the edge gives a definite eye. (Left) White captures Black; Black will retake immediately in a snapback. (Right) The position after Black retakes with the marked stone. Black has two eyes.

5.6 From one space to two eyes?

It was back on p.10 that this idea was first mentioned. A space of three or more points may often be divided into two eyes.

There are half a dozen basic shapes every Go player has to know and recognize, in which a well-chosen play in the centre of a larger eye makes two eyes, or prevents their formation. This is the one topic any introductory book on Go ought to cover in detail. You will certainly win and lose many games just on your understanding of the small number of facts on the next few pages. You can study this section with advantage as early on in your Go career as you like. It is placed here as a matter of logical order.

Three-point spaces

There are two patterns.

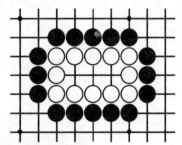

First, three points in a line.

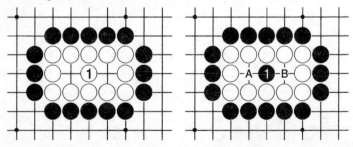

White makes two eyes by playing in the middle (**left**). Black can play there (**right**), and then White can do nothing. After Black 1, Black can play at A. If White captures two stones with B, Black plays back inside, White captures, and Black recaptures all the White stones (just as on p.8).

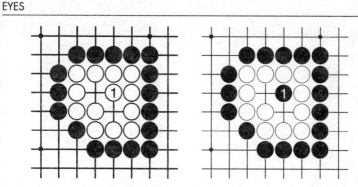

The other pattern has three points in an L-shape. It goes the same way. White lives by playing at the centre. If Black plays there, White is dead.

Four-point spaces

There are essentially five shapes to look at with four points in them.

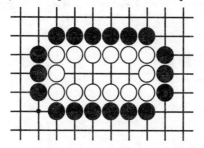

With four points in a line White is already alive. White should not add another stone to this group.

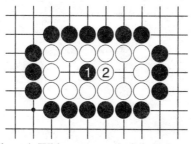

If Black plays inside at 1, White answers at 2 for two eyes. If Black at 2, White plays at 1. The other Black plays need no answer.

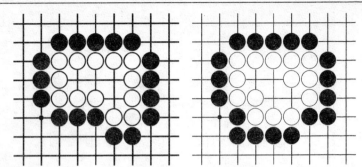

These two patterns are alive, just like the straight line.

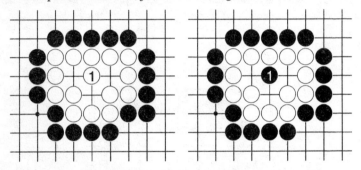

In the fourth case of a T-shape, White plays in the centre to live. Black plays at the same point to kill White. (See also p.86.)

Five-point spaces

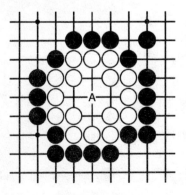

The number of shapes increases with the number of spaces. But from now on most of them are alive. This cross shape is one with five spaces, for which White needs to play at A to live. Naturally Black plays there to kill White, too.

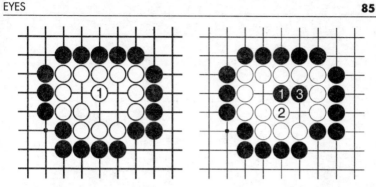

This is the other, more interesting case of a shape that might die. It has various names: 'hatchet five', 'bulky five'. White lives by playing at 1. Black can kill White by playing there, too.

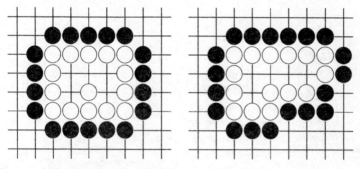

These and all other shapes with five spaces are alive.

Spaces of six and more points

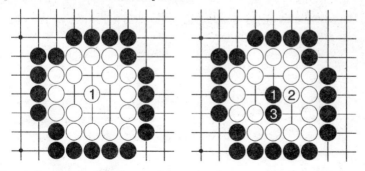

Here is just one further shape, 'flower six', in which Black can kill White.

5.7 Status

You might have noticed the absence of this shape, with four spaces, from the list of shapes given in 5.6.

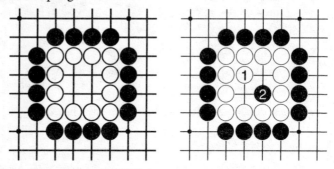

The fact is that it falls into a category different from all the others that were considered there. It is simply dead. If White tries to make two eyes with 1, Black plays 2.

It is very helpful, in dealing with life and death questions on the Go board, to introduce the idea of *status* of a group. We have now met the three fundamental examples: a group may be dead as it stands; it may be unsettled – meaning it can be killed, or be made to live, depending on whose turn it is; or it may be alive (whoever plays first).

Summary of the eye status of standard shapes

Dead groups include those with just one eye, or no eye . The 2x2 square shape above is an example.

Unsettled groups include those that can make two eyes with just one more play, but may also be killed. The shapes with three spaces, the T-shape of four spaces, the cross and 'bulky' shapes of five, and the 'flower' shape of six spaces from 5.6 are examples.

Live groups include those which are alive whatever the opponent tries. The three shapes from 5.6 with four spaces are examples. The many other shapes not mentioned with more spaces fall into this category.

5.8 A shape's status can change

The examples given in 5.6 were all presented with the basic shape surrounded by a single White chain. There was a good reason for this. It is important to realize that the presence of cutting points, or proximity to the edge, can change the status of a group based on a standard shape.

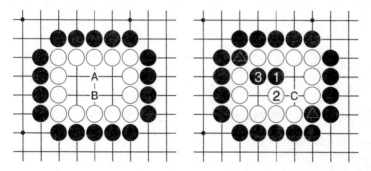

For example, six points in a rectangle. The shape **(left)** is alive – White can play one of A and B if Black plays the other. It is helpful to think of this as a normal size for an eye space that makes a live group. But with two cutting points **(right)**, introduced by the marked Black stones, it becomes unsettled. After Black 3 there is a snapback (Black at C). White can do nothing about this. If White connects at C the group is dead.

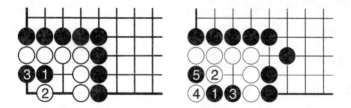

(Left) In the corner the same shape is unsettled even without cutting points. White is dead after Black 3.

(Right) Even with an extra liberty outside, it becomes a kind of *ko* fight, to be classified in its proper place in a later chapter (p.115).

There are some more examples of this kind given in the problems on p.95.

5.9 Half eyes

There is another fundamental way to make two eyes. You make one eye in one place, and one eye in another. You can say that the techniques of the last three sections are right for *short, fat* groups. Then you want to make two eyes in one place. But many groups are *long, thin* groups. In fact any group that has to run away because it hasn't enough eye space is what is called a *weak* group; and weak groups tend to become long and thin exactly because they must escape, avoiding being shut in.

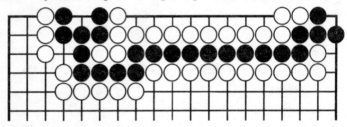

This Black group is alive. That should be clear – two eyes far apart.

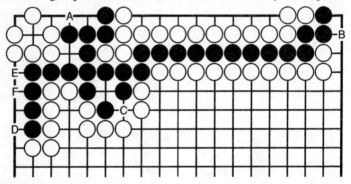

How about this one? Yes, it is alive. There are four moves for Black to make one eye: A, B, C, D. If White starts attacking then Black will still be able to play two of these points, and make two eyes. Of course, if Black plays D then White E must be answered by Black F to make the eye.

A *half eye* means a place where you can make an eye. Four half eyes are enough to live. More usual is to make an eye and two halves. Another related remark is that an unsettled eye shape is 'one and a half eyes': connected to an additional half eye it makes a live group (see problem 13, p.94).

For example, here is an easy problem. Black to play and live.

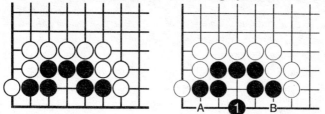

Black plays at the centre, making an eye and two half eyes. Black will be able to play either at A or at B to make a second eye.

Here are some more examples of half eyes, considered in isolation.

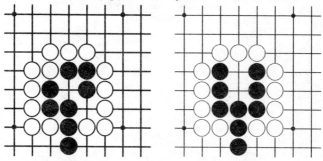

It is quite difficult to build an eye in the centre.

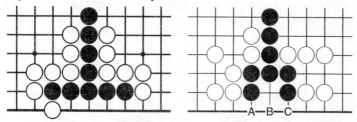

On the right here, Black makes an eye with A, B or C. White can take it away only with B.

The half eye concept is a natural combination of the status idea of 5.7, and the way of breaking up the Go board into parts talked about in 2.5. Anyone who considers the eye status of part of a group will come to think in terms of half eyes. If you are counting half eyes, you must take care that the places they occupy are truly independent locations for potential eyes, not coupled in some subtle way.

5.10 False eyes and snapback

Knowledge about eye shape is useful not only for understanding the life
and death of groups, but also because it affects any kind of fighting in a
game of Go that depends on numbers of liberties. That means the idea of a
false eye is far more generally important. Go players tend to talk about
shape. It seems to be a well-kept secret that eye shape is a major part of
that subject.

To make the point, we compare the four types of false eye mentioned in 5.2
with the four kinds of snapback from Chapter 3.

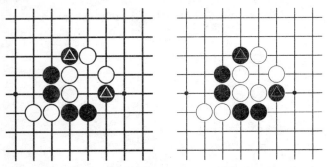

This is taken from p.41. By marking the two Black stones in the eye-
stealing relationship, it is made much more obvious how the mechanism of
the snapback works. Black gives White a stone. But White gains a false
eye by capturing it (**right**), not an eye. White's chain loses a liberty in
capturing, and Black can take it back.

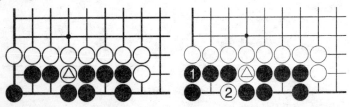

Here is another example, matching the way the marked White stone destroys
Black's eye in the corner to the third kind of snapback on p.41. Looking
back, the second kind of snapback on that same page was of a clamp type:
it corresponds to the clamping method of making an eye false from p.77.
The last type of snapback (problem 11 on p.45) matches the fourth kind of
false eye, in the corner, from p.78.

The point of all this classification isn't to be tidy-minded. It is to help you learn to avoid some disasters on the board.

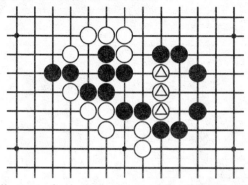

This looks like part of a typical game position. White has lost the three marked stones in earlier fighting. Black probably believes White has no way to rescue them.

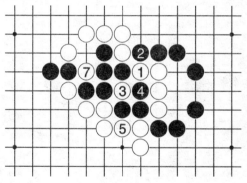

In fact White can save them (Black 6 at 3). White 3 threatens a snapback of eye-stealing type, and White 7 is a clamp snapback.

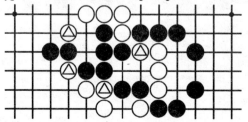

Just enough of the position again, with the key stones marked.

5.11 False eye liberties

It can be said that *a false eye liberty loses a liberty*. This idea applies in the situations on this page.

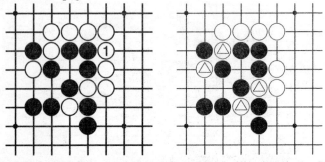

Here is quite a simple example, though possibly still a surprise to Black. White can capture three Black stones with a play at 1. The eye-stealing relationships behind this are marked **(right)**.

To make the same point in a different way, here's an artificial position to finish off the chapter. Black has been given one of each kind of false eye.

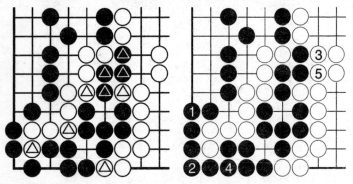

(Left) The key White stones are marked. It may look as if White has lost a chain of ten stones inside Black's territory, but in fact there is a capturing race going on. You should be able to see that White is well ahead in this race, and will be able to capture the marked Black chain of four stones first.

(Right) Analysing the position more deeply, you can see that Black 1 isn't a threat to the White chain. Black is more than one move behind in the race. Even when Black has played 2 and 4 White can win the fight.

5.12 Problems

To improve, it is important to solve life and death problems like these, especially easy ones typical of simple positions from games. Real games and real examples, like real lives, are more messy than the books say. Still, this understanding is important to develop, firstly through clear-cut cases.

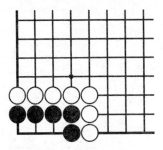
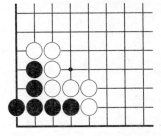

1,2. White to play and kill Black.

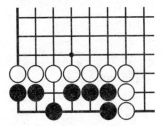
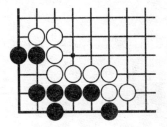

3,4. White to play and kill Black.

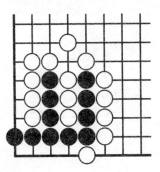
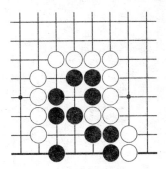

5,6. Black to play and live.

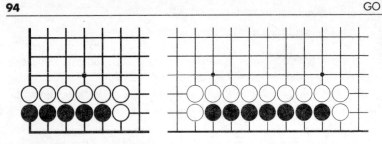

7,8. White to play and kill.

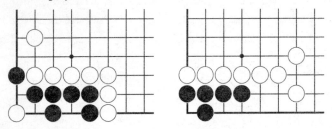

9. (Left) Black to play and live. **10. (Right)** White to play and kill.

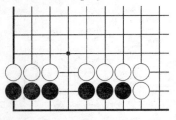
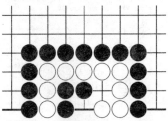

11. (Left) White to play. **12. (Right)** If Black ever needs to capture the White stones, because of an external capturing race, where to play?

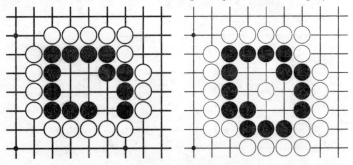

13. (Left) Black to play and live. **14. (Right)** Status of the Black group?

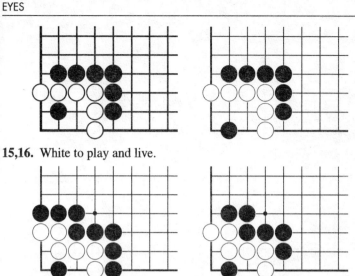

15,16. White to play and live.

17,18. White to play. What is the result in the two cases?

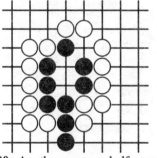 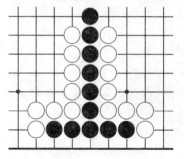

19,20. Are these eyes or half eyes for Black?

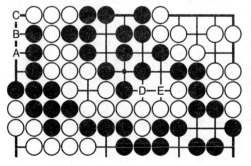

21. Taken from a real game; Black has better eye shape than White has. Which of the plays A to E win the capturing race for Black?

5.13 Solutions

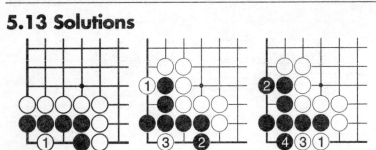

1. (Left) White kills Black. **2. (Centre)** White kills Black. **(Right)** White fails, Black has two eyes.

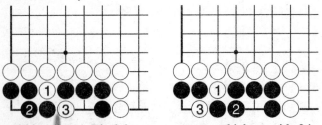

3. After White plays 1, Black loses some stones whichever side 2 is.

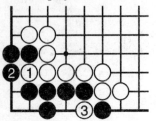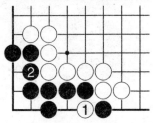

4. White plays as on the left. The right-hand line leaves Black alive.

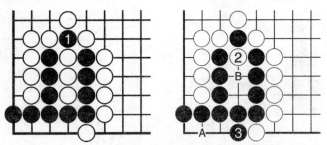

5. Black captures, and if White 2 then Black 3 leaves A or B to live.

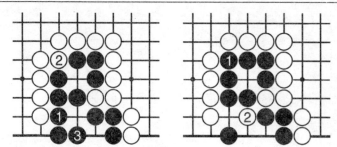

6. Black can live (**left**), but mustn't try to save all the stones.
(**Right**) Black dies, trying to save the three stones in the centre.

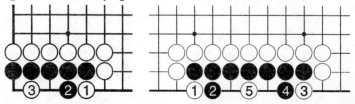

7,8. Attrition. White kills Black by limiting the eye space from outside first, then playing in the centre. Black only gains false eyes by taking the White pieces on the edge.

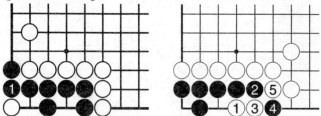

9. (Left) Black should play at 1. If White plays there, the eye becomes false.
10. (Right) When White plays at 1, Black can capture two stones. But then White plays back at 3, to give Black a false eye.

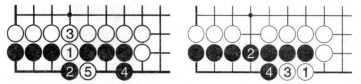

11. The key point is White 1 in the left-hand diagram. Black dies. If White starts as in the right-hand diagram, Black lives.

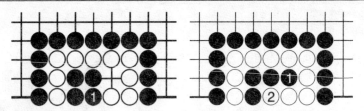

12. If Black really must take White's stones off the board, it is important to start by making the 2x2 shape **(left)**. If Black makes the L-shape, White captures at 2 and makes a live shape **(right)**.

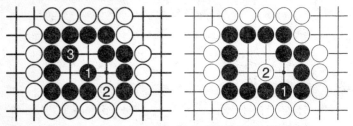

13. (Left) Black must play 1 here to live. **(Right)** Black dies.

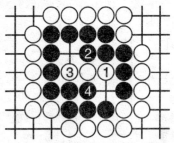

14. This Black group is alive (status), but is a *seki* whoever starts (p.121).

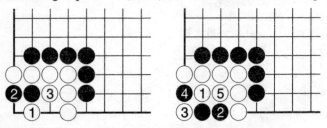

15. When White has two liberties on the outside, life is easy.
16. In the right-hand diagram, White 5 prevents any *ko* fight.

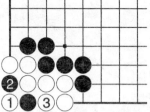

17. (Left) White must settle for a *ko*. **18. (Right)** With two extra liberties on the outside White plays 1 and 3, and is completely alive.

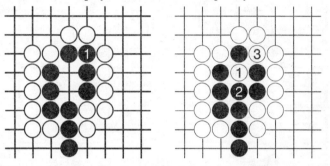

19. This is a half eye. Black can complete the eye, White can destroy it with a throw-in trick.

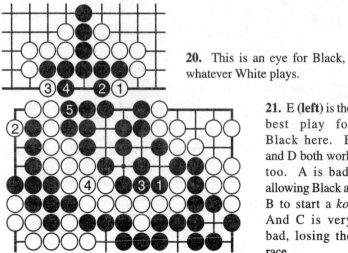

20. This is an eye for Black, whatever White plays.

21. E **(left)** is the best play for Black here. B and D both work too. A is bad, allowing Black at B to start a *ko*. And C is very bad, losing the race.

6 | A COMPLETE GAME

6.1 Starting out

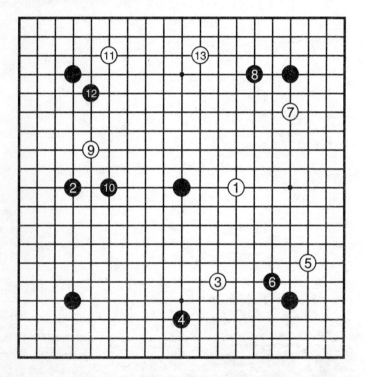

(1–13) This is one of my teaching games. The unmarked Black stones are the handicap, placed on the board before White starts. White plays unconventional moves. Black answers well, taking good points with 2 and 4, and avoiding getting shut in with 6 and 12.

Variations from the game are shown in smaller diagrams. The numbering in them starts again from 1. See the box on p.6 also.

6.2 Fighting begins

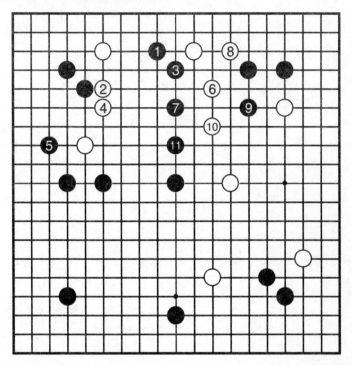

(1–11) Black invades on the top side, a forceful way to play. White has difficulties in saving both the stones played there. White 2 and 4 threaten to shut in the top left corner, but Black 5 helps it.

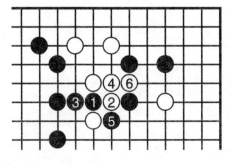

Beginners tend to be nervous of the one-point jump. White 10 is quite safe. Black cannot gain by the wedge (**left**). Here White 6 sets up a connection or double *atari* play. In the game Black's jumps 7 and 11 are good, too.

6.3 Eruption of a *ko* battle

(1–22) White deals with the problem of defending in the upper left by starting a *ko*. First 1, 3 and 5 leave Black short of liberties, and then 7 aims at the weak points at 17 and 18. Black should have kept the peep 12 in reserve as a *ko* threat.

This is not a long *ko* fight. White uses 17 as a threat, and then recaptures with 19 (at the point 9). Black 20 and 22 are very damaging to the other White group, but White finishes the *ko* at once by capturing Black with 21.

The left-hand White group is now strong. It has two obvious eyes, and chances of a further attack against the Black corner. The two White stones cut off on the top side by 20 and 22 may become useful later, but for the moment White doesn't try to make them live.

The cutting point below 5 also has to wait for attention. At present White can give up the two stones including 3 if Black cuts.

6.4 The lower left and right

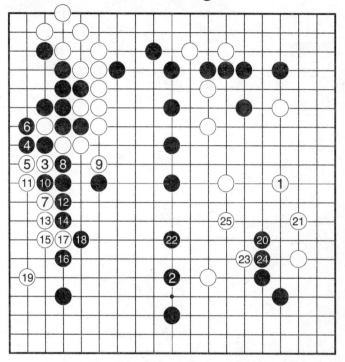

(1–25) White holds the initiative, and uses it to reinforce the right side. A Black invasion here would be difficult for White to cope with, now that Black is strong in the upper right.

Black builds up the lower left with 2. This is good. White hasn't yet played any stone in that quarter of the board.

Black makes some mistakes as White plays on the left side. With 4, Black should capture cleanly at 6. Black 10 reduces the liberties on the chain, without good reason. And Black 16 lets White make two cutting points in Black's shape.

At the end of this diagram, it still looks as if Black might make 40 points in the lower left. Added to 30 in prospect in the upper right, and up to 10 in the upper left, this makes 80 for Black. White might make 20 on the right side, 10 on the left side, and 10 in the upper left. Black is ahead by 40.

6.5 Black tries too hard

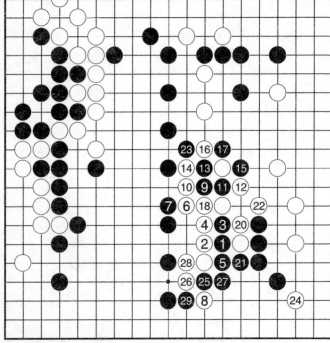

(1–29) In this figure Black 19 connects, one point above 11.

Black shows a determination to fight all out. When White jumps down to 8 Black's lower right corner seems to be cut off. However, Black had clearly prepared the wedge at 25 to meet that eventuality. What we shall see next is that the large Black territory to the left is affected.

The count of the game given on the previous page shows that Black was in no need of a further capture of White stones with 23. So it would have been better for Black to have defended the lower right corner against the 3–3 invasion which comes with White 24 (more about this in 9.1). As it is, the game runs out of control. It is very much to the stronger player's advantage to have a handicap game become a matter of Black fire-fighting.

Note that White has consistently made large and small sacrifices. White 22, allowing Black to capture two stones, is a connection, since White could take back at once.

6.6 A bush fire

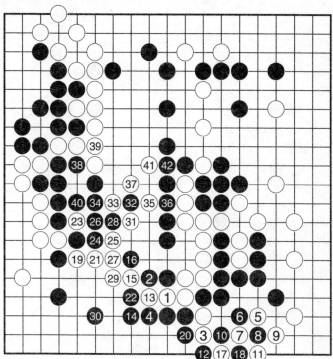

(1–42) In this figure White makes use of weaknesses in the lower left quarter of the board to break in and reduce Black's territory there. This deals with the most pressing strategic issue, as far as White is concerned. At the end of these plays the endgame will start.

The sequence is sparked off by Black's difficulties in the lower right. Another *ko* fight arises there after 17. Black ignores White's threat at 19, to make sure, with 20, of the capture of the two awkward White stones.

White has many threats, and puts them together to cut into Black's area. Black even has to play 40 to make two eyes. Rather than trying to analyse some of the many possibilities, let's point out the major gains for White:

■ Black has lost territory on the left.

■ White has an established group in the lower right corner.

■ White has retained the initiative.

6.7 Into the endgame

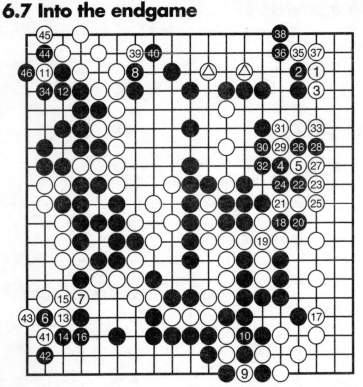

(1–46) Quite suddenly the game has entered a fresh phase. To be in the endgame means that large scale fighting, and major issues of life and death, are no longer on the agenda. This doesn't, however, mean that tactics are redundant.

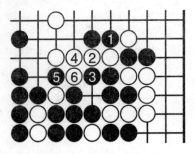

For example, why not Black 30 at 31? The reason is that the 'dead' White stones still have some life left in them (left). Both players had to consider the effect of the marked White stones on the upper side, too.

6.8 Finishing off

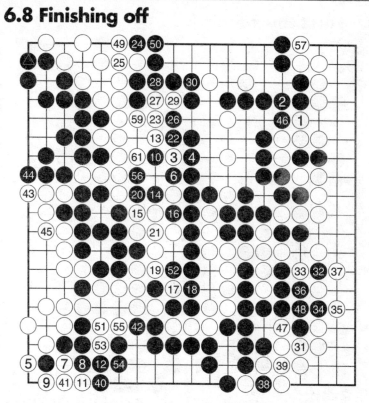

(1–62) The end of an arduous game. Black 58 took the *ko* left of 17, Black 60 filled it. The last play was Black 62, filling the *ko* left of 38. White might have started a further and risky *ko* (but didn't wish to), at the point with the triangle Black stone on it, which was therefore eventually filled by Black as if it were a neutral point.

White won this game by three points, having pulled ahead only in the course of the endgame. The detailed counting is explained on the next page. There were many mistakes (on both sides). However, it represents Go, the fighting game. Tactics continued into this diagram. For example, please work out why Black 2, here, can't be played at 46.

The game was close, because in a series of games my opponent and I had adjusted the handicap to make it tough on both of us. The handicap system is one of the major attractions of Go.

6.9 Final touches

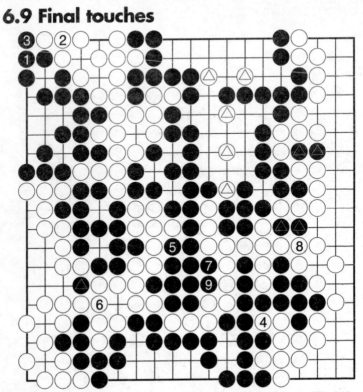

This diagram shows how the neutral points might have been filled (1 to 9). White obviously has to play inside at 2 and 8, but also at 6 as well to avoid a snapback tactic.

The hopeless pieces the players would give up as dead, but only after filling the neutral points, are marked with triangles. There are five for each side. The prisoners, already off the board, were 12 White taken by Black, and nine Black taken by White.

Black's territories can be counted as nine points in the top left, two points in the lower centre, 13 points on the lower side, and 37 on the upper side, making a total of 61. Including 17 prisoners, Black's score comes to 78.

White has four points in the upper left, 16 in the lower left, and 47 on the right side, for a total of 67. Together with a total of 14 prisoners that makes a score of 81 for White. The margin in the game was a slender three points.

7 | KO AND *SEKI*

You need only read 7.1, 7.2 and 7.3 of this chapter first time through. You can use the other sections for reference, and read them as required.

7.1 *Kos arise naturally*

The possibility of *ko* fights adds greatly to the difficulty of Go, but also to its interest. *Kos* can be involved in each of the skills of Chapters 3, 4 and 5. *Ko* makes the status concept of 5.7 more complex, too.

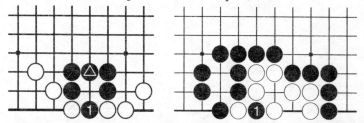

(Left) A *ko* can arise, for Black to cut White, based on the marked stone.
(Right) This *ko* holds the key to the life or death of the White group.

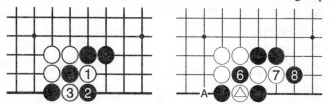

Let's follow the *ko* fight on p.34 a little way. Black 4 is elsewhere on the board (a *ko* threat, trying to compel White to answer); and we suppose White responds. Then back to Black 6. White 7 is a *local* threat: one that must be answered before fighting on. If Black answers by connecting where the marked White stone was, White plays at A. So Black needs to play 8. White 17 on p.102 is another example of a local *ko* threat.

7.2 Recognizing *ko*

The *ko* examples in 7.1 were all of *ko* fights on the edge. These are very common. Make sure that you can recognize all the usual *ko* situations, and other possibilities, by working through this page.

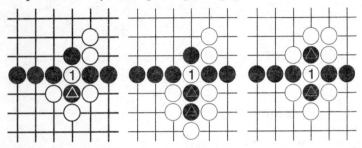

Left to right: a real *ko* fight in which White tries to cut Black in the centre; not a *ko* because White takes two Black stones, then Black recaptures White to connect; not a *ko* because White captures two Black stones (and then Black is cut).

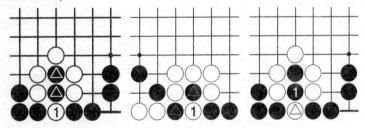

To compare with the *kos* on the edge from 7.1. **Left to right:** White captures two, then Black can recapture (cf. problem 2 on p.68); White captures two and Black can't recapture; a snapback as seen in 3.9. None of these is *ko*.

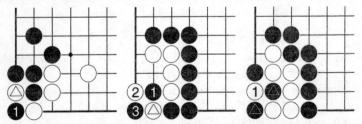

Two *kos* right in the corner, and (**right**) a capture of two Black stones.

7.3 *Kos* and decision making

Ko fights are part of 'living Go', and are best studied in positions from real games. Playing a *ko* properly may be a very testing example for the count/read/decide paradigm of 2.5. To apply this method well is a sign of near-professional level.

One type of decision has to do with how important the *ko* fight is. Extreme cases are:

- **The all-dominating *ko*:** Whoever wins the *ko* by controlling the two intersections at its centre will win the game (see 7.5).
- **The picnic *ko*:** One player will suffer great loss by losing the *ko*, the other player will lose very little (the second example in 7.1 is a picnic *ko* for Black).
- **The half-point *ko*:** Worth only one point to the winner (for example the final plays in 6.8), so not important to either player.

These types are quite easy to recognize, but in most other cases some counting is necessary to assess the value of the *ko*, and threats.

Another sort of decision is 'choice of exit' from a *ko*. It is easy to continue in a *ko* fight beyond the point at which one should do something else. A *ko* fight is a cycle of six plays:

- one player, say Black, takes the *ko*;
- White makes a play other than the recapture, a '*ko* threat';
- Black answers White's threat;
- White retakes the *ko*;
- Black makes a *ko* threat;
- White answers Black's threat,

and at this point Black can retake the *ko*. This brings the players back to the start of the cycle. Black has three ways to break out of the cycle. If Black does not answer White's threat, then Black can finish the *ko* (by connecting in it, or by capturing or playing in a way that removes the *ko* formation); or sometimes plays to make the *ko* more important. This is called ignoring a *ko* threat. But there are two other exits. After White retakes, Black can make a play not intended as a threat. Or Black can abandon fighting the *ko*, by not retaking. These options may be more sensible if the *ko* isn't so important, or can't be won; or to save *ko* threats.

7.4 Management of *ko* threats

A second difficult feature of *kos* is that there are special techniques associated with the proper management of *ko* threats. A decision to ignore a *ko* threat from your opponent which has a damaging follow-up play will always be hard. Much better to have more threats yourself.

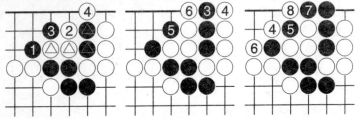

Most interesting from a tactical point of view is to find extra *ko* threats by playing skilfully. Here is an example from the position to be seen on the next page. Black has a chance of *ko* threats using the two marked Black stones in the left-hand diagram. These are certainly captured by White in a chase down. But they have some life left in them, and can be used to make threats against White's two marked stones. What Black did was to play 1 and 3 for two threats **(left)**. Black 3 should have been played to the edge **(centre)** – Black would have had an extra threat at 5. **(Right)** If White then plays 4 wrongly, even more. In general, play threats so as to leave further threats in the same area, and answer them to avoid this.

It isn't true that you have to play threats in decreasing order of value. Here is some further advice on managing *ko* threats:

- ■ Set up *kos* in which you are the first to capture.
- ■ Shun *ko* threats that lose points (all threats lose chances).
- ■ Threats to start another *ko* are smaller than they may look.
- ■ Threats that are very big can be kept for a later fight.
- ■ Only local threats (7.1) matter in all-dominating *kos* (7.3).
- ■ *Ko* threats for both sides are mythical creatures: if the opponent leaves them to you, play them all out, then take.
- ■ It can be useful to make the opponent use a threat by capturing a *ko* once, then exit yourself.
- ■ A *ko* in a capturing race should normally be taken late on.
- ■ Above all, don't waste *ko* threats by playing forcing moves that aren't necessary, at any stage of the game.

7.5 The real McKoy

Here is a *ko* fight from a real game (another teaching game of mine).

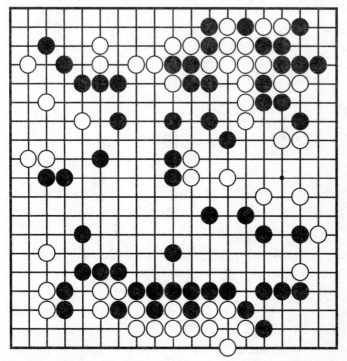

This is the position, with White to play. A rough count of the game is informative. White has about 50 points round the edges. Black has played many stones to construct influence in the centre of the board. This was a five stone handicap game, in the same series as the one in Chapter 6. Very often in a handicap game White finds it easy to invade and make groups with third line territory in them. Then Black has to use the fourth line walls properly (cf. p.19). Often Black's resulting influence dominates the centre.

A count of Black's territory, on the assumption that the centre yields as many points as it appears, White just pushing in from outside, shows that Black would have about 70 points. White takes note of this. The plan must be to break into the centre.

Note that White did not have to count very accurately to see this.

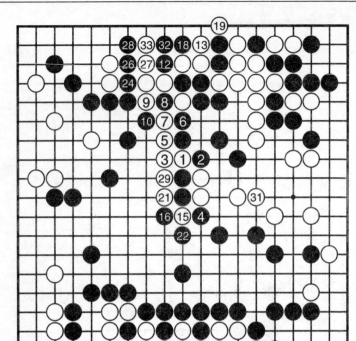

(1–33) This is what happened in the game, ending in Black's resignation. A *ko* fight which was all-dominating arose after Black 10. The plays 11, 14, 17, 20 and 23 were *ko* captures at the points 8 or 9. White 25 was at 8, ending the *ko*. Black 30 was at 15. This was a regular *ko* fight as explained in 7.3, with a six play cycle; and all the *ko* threats were local to the fight, a bullet point in 7.4.

It was explained in 7.4 that Black didn't handle the *ko* threats on the top side perfectly. Meanwhile White was manufacturing *ko* threats in the centre with 15 and 21. Black 4 at the point 15, giving up a point of territory but avoiding a serious cutting point, would have been a better idea.

There is plenty of study material here. Why did White play 31? You should be able to discover that without it the Black stones in the centre can escape. Should Black have played 16 at 21? If Black ignores the threat 21 to connect the *ko*, who wins?

7.6 Types of *ko*

This is a reference section. There are many more types of *ko* than have been seen so far. Some of them have effects on the game that mean they are the subject of rulings, additions to the small set of rules that governs almost all Go games. All of them present complications in the status concept of 5.7, meaning that to make a complete list of the possible status of groups is too long a job for most players. The problem occurs also if you try to list possible outcomes of capturing races.

'Rulings' sounds unpleasant. This is the traditional way of explaining extra rules in Japan. The first successful codification dates back only to 1989. Some groups with complex status are said to be alive or dead at the end of a game. Some games with repeating positions are annulled – treated as draws, and played again if between pros in Japan. And some positions are treated as a *seki*.

Indirect *ko*

This means a *ko* in a capturing race, in which one side must ignore more than one *ko* threat in order to win the race.

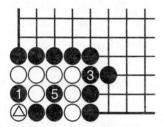 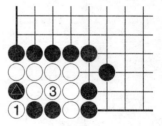

This example came up on p.87.

In the left-hand diagram, what Black can achieve by taking White in the *ko* in the corner (Black 1), ignoring a White *ko* threat, and playing at 3 to fill a White liberty, is to set up a direct (normal) *ko*. Then, in that *ko* fight, if Black ignores a further *ko* threat and plays at 5, Black captures the White corner. On the right, White can live just by ignoring one Black *ko* threat and capturing with 3.

Making a balance sheet, on the left Black makes 16 points in total; on the right White makes 6 points. That's a swing of 22 points, but with a difference of three plays elsewhere.

Kos in sequence

This means that there is a *ko* in which one of the players may ignore a *ko* threat and go on to a second *ko* capture.

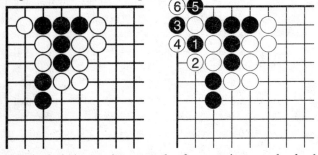

Here is a particularly interesting example of a capturing race that leads to a *ko*. Filling White's liberties more slowly will fail for Black. The cut at 1 looks very poor, but after 2 and 3 it will be a *ko*. There is a variation at this point (problem 6, p.122). In the line shown, how can Black win the race?

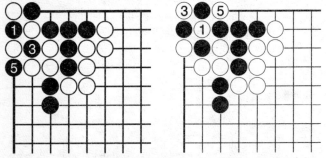

Black can win by playing 1, 3 and 5 in a row (**left**). At the point when Black has played 3, but not 5, White has a similar task (**right**) but going in the other direction. The fight may rage back and forth.

Terminology varies.

- The admirable James Davies in his book *Life and Death* (Kiseido) calls an indirect *ko* a multi-step *ko*, and a sequence like this a multi-stage *ko*.
- Jin Jiang's *Fighting Ko* (Yutopian) uses 'approach move' (also 'wayward') *ko* for the former, multi-step for the latter.
- The Japanese call an indirect *ko* an endgame *ko*, to emphasize the usually low value of plays in it.

Double *ko*

The effect of two *kos* in one fight may be to cut or connect, to kill, to make life, or to construct a kind of *seki*, to decide a capturing race.

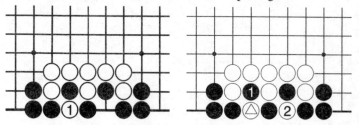

It is pointless for Black to try to connect along the edge here, once White has taken **(left)**. However many *ko* threats Black has, White can always take in the other *ko* when Black retakes **(right)**.

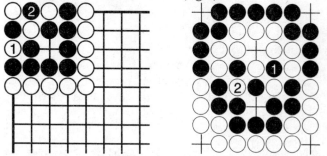

(Left) Black has an eye, White doesn't. White cannot capture Black. But this corner serves as an unlimited source of *ko* threats for White.

Ruling: The White stones are hopeless, and are taken off at the end.

(Right) In this different situation, each side has an eye.

Ruling: Treated as a *seki* (no points for either) at the end of the game.

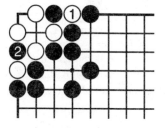

White can never control both points required to make a second eye. But White has an unlimited supply of *ko* threats here.

Ruling: Dead. The White stones are removed at the end of the game.

Triple *ko*

If there are three *kos* in a game that can be taken in a cycle, and neither player is prepared to concede two of the three to the opponent, it is possible for a game position to repeat. Note that the simple presence of three *kos* on the board doesn't constitute a triple *ko*. For example, with three half-point *kos* all that is at stake is whether you connect one or two of them – just one point. A triple *ko* occurs less than once in a thousand games, perhaps once in a playing career.

Ruling: Such a game is annulled. (Often this is counted as a draw in amateur competitions, but Japanese pros have to play the game again.)

The simplest kind of triple *ko* to imagine is like this: a big capturing race with no liberties left besides in three *kos* between the chains. The 1998 Meijin match had one of a different type: a double *ko* providing unlimited threats for both players, plus a second *ko* neither could concede.

Bent four in the corner

A common type of life and death position, and a frequently applied ruling.

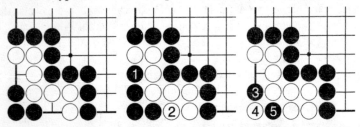

This is a more subtle version of the L-shaped four-space problem (problem17 from p.95). In this case, too, Black can start a *ko*, as shown. *Black can wait indefinitely to do so*. The possibility can be latent through much of a game.
Ruling: White's group is dead, and may be taken off at the end of the game.

Therefore this position isn't at all the *seki* it may appear to be, at first sight. White's only chance is to attack Black's wall, forcing Black to start the *ko*.

Postponed *kos,* ten thousand year *ko*

The two names imply a *ko* that both players would be glad to defer almost indefinitely. A ruling is needed in case it never starts, to explain how to count.

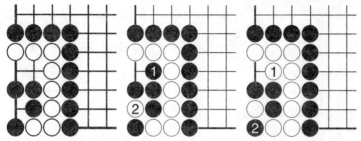

This is a strange position, but of a type arising naturally in life and death problems, and found in capturing races too. Both players can mix it up. Black can play 1 (**centre**) when the position becomes a direct *ko*. White can fight an indirect *ko* (**right**), filling a liberty while ignoring a *ko* threat. Black can at any time connect the *ko* in the left-hand position, making a *seki*.

Ruling: Treated as a *seki*, when it persists to the end of the game.

Some players would reserve the term 'ten thousand year *ko*' for this type of position, but in which the *ko* is indirect for both players.

That exhausts the list of *kos,* anomalous positions and rulings needed by anyone not intending to become a Go rules wizard.

7.7 Two sorts of *seki*

An example of a *seki* was seen on p.14. It is no good trying to show all types of *seki*. In a capturing race one of three things will happen in the long run:

- Matters will be resolved, with a winner and a loser.
- The players continue playing, and the position repeats.
- The players stop playing in the area voluntarily.

Seki is a general name for the third case in this classification. This possibility gives rise to '*seki* as *impasse*' – a capturing race leading to a blocked position. A second type, 'eye shape *seki*', is a possible resolution of a life and death problem. It is quite different. It doesn't depend on the number of outside liberties. But it is rather sensitive to cutting points.

Seki as impasse

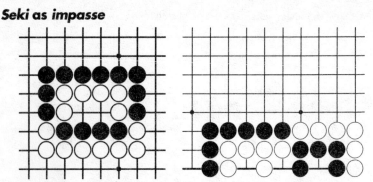

In positions such as these it is clear enough why neither player plays on, filling in a liberty in the area between the two inside chains. That would simply mean immediate capture.

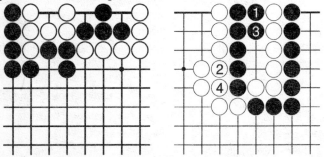

Seki will not happen between a chain with an eye, and a chain without an eye. **(Left)** Black has lost the capturing race. Some positions will result in a *seki* even if one player starts ahead in liberties. **(Right)** Black starts two liberties ahead of White – but still a *seki*.

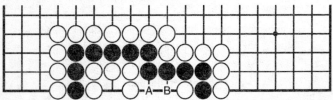

What will happen in this position? Such situations can arise from speculative invasions towards the end of a game.

Black should play at B. Then it is a *seki*. White should play at A, not B. Then Black can capture at B – but that's a snapback.

Eye shape *seki*

The other type of *seki* that matters in practice, has one player able to capture the other, but not willing to, because that would make an unsettled or dead eye shape, in the sense of 5.7.

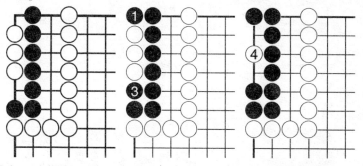

We have deliberately given Black many external liberties, to emphasize the point that this isn't a straight capturing race. Black can capture White. It is just that it is a very bad idea. White will then kill Black with 4.

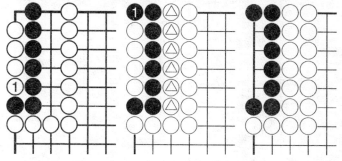

Equally, it is absurd for White to play inside. Right at the end, when White has filled six marked neutral points, Black takes White for a living shape.

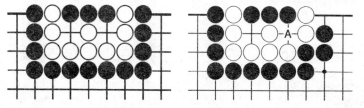

(**Left**) This is a *seki*. (**Right**) Here White is dead, since Black can force White to play at A. White can do nothing.

7.8 Problems

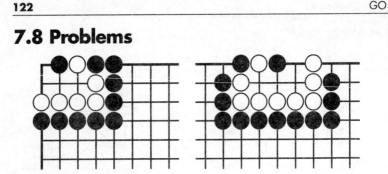

1,2. White to play. Is it *ko* for White to live?

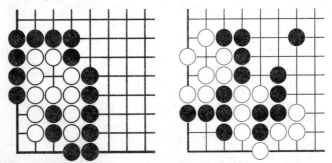

3. (Left) Black to play and kill. **4. (Right)** Black to play and live.

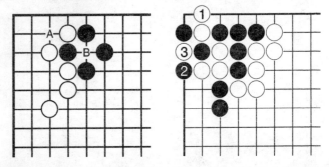

5. (Left) Black has just ignored a White *ko* threat, and will play again here. What are the relative merits of the plays at A and B?

6. (Right) In this position from p.116 White has chosen to set up a direct *ko*, rather than the sequence of two *kos* for Black shown there. What possible advantage could this have?

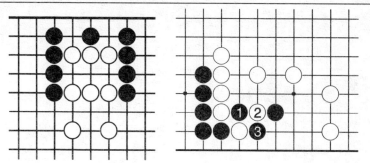

7. (Left) White can use *ko* to break Black's connection. **8. (Right)** What results here after Black 3?

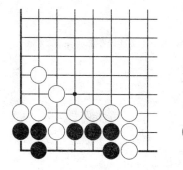

9,10. Black to play and avoid *ko*.

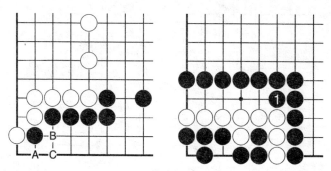

11. (Left) Is Black's correct play here A, B or C?

12. (Right) This is a capturing race. What is the correct way to play here for White? How important is it to answer Black?

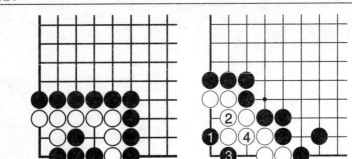

13,14. What is the status of these White corner positions?

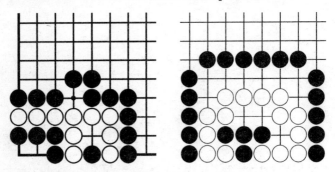

15,16. What is the status of these White positions?

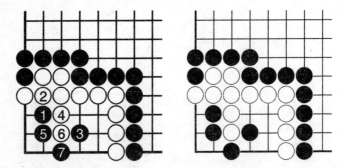

17. Black has played an invasion of White's corner, beginning with the peep at 1. In the resulting position, on the right, Black would be glad to make a *seki,* so that White would score no points here. How can White prevent this?

7.9 Solutions

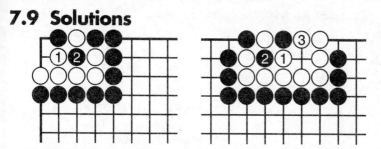

1. (Left) White must play for a *ko* to live. **2. (Right)** White lives without *ko*. If Black plays 2 at 3 White simply captures one stone to live.

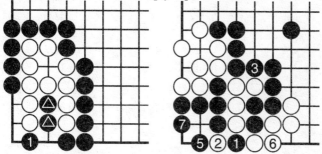

3. (Left) Black kills White by sacrificing the two marked stones, and retaking. **4. (Right)** White plays 4 at 1 and Black lives; but the *ko* would be interesting in a game. It arises if 3 were at 5, and White played 4 at 7.

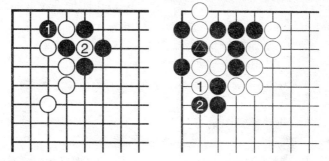

5. (Left) Choice A shown as 1 here is the way for Black to increase the value of the *ko*. The choice of connection at B is good only to make territory on the top side. **6. (Right)** This alternative way of playing the *ko* has the advantage for White of a local *ko* threat at 1.

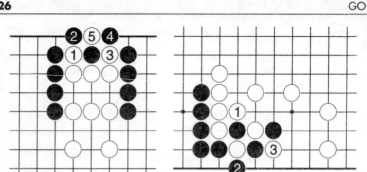

7. (Left) White has a *ko*. **8. (Right)** After White 3, a *ko* fight arises here.

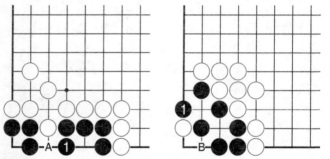

9. (Left) Black plays at 1 and is alive, since White cannot cut with A. If Black plays at A instead, a *ko* results when White plays at 1.

10. (Right) Black has to counter the threat of a *ko* set up with White B, and White's threat to connect along the edge. Black 1 is the way to proceed.

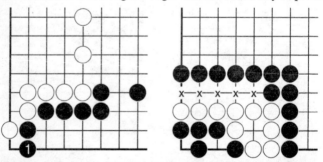

11. (Left) This is the correct endgame play, avoiding a *ko* after White at A.
12. (Right) This very indirect *ko* results when White takes three stones and Black takes them back. With many liberties White can wait to answer here.

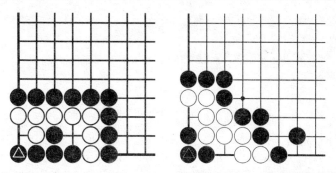

13. (Left) If neither player starts the *ko* in the corner, it is treated as a *seki*. Black can play the marked stone to be sure of that result. (See p.119.)

14. (Right) This corner is dead, by the bent four ruling (p.118). Imagine the marked stone in position. (White can do nothing about it.)

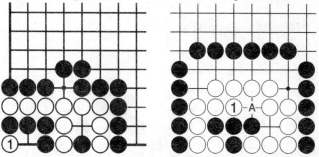

15. (Left) Unsettled. White to play can live at 1. Black to play kills White by filling the outside liberty. A *seki* cannot occur. **16. (Right)** Unsettled. White lives in a *seki* by playing at 1. Black kills White, playing there and then eventually A for the 'flower six' shape.

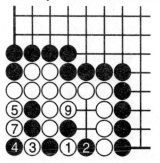

17. White avoids trouble here with a careful sequence of throw-in plays. First White 1 and then White 3 set up a situation in which Black loses the capturing race inside. Black 6 is at 3, Black 8 at 1. If Black 2 is at 3 then White plays at 2 and wins the capturing race.

8 | THE END OF
THE GAME

The beginner very often finds the end of a game of Go to be the hardest phase. One of the difficulties is that it comes by agreement; and one must understand what it is one is agreeing. Another problem is that endgame positions may require the full range of Go tactics. It is for this reason that this chapter is placed at the end of the series dealing with tactical fundamentals.

8.1 Neutral points

One way to try to make the last part of the game more comprehensible is to start at the far end. The final stage is to fill the neutral points.

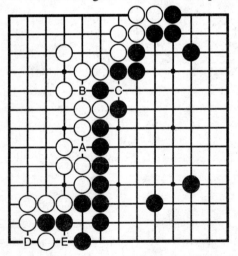

At the end of this quiet game, there are five neutral points. Either side may play at A. White B must be answered by Black C. Black must play at E when White plays at D, to avoid losing a point.

A very important Japanese Go term is *sente* (pronounced 'sen-tay'), meaning 'retaining the initiative'. For the most part such terms have been avoided in this book, with accepted English equivalents used instead. But *sente*, and its opposite *gote* (pronounced 'goh-tay', and meaning 'losing the initiative') are indispensible. The endgame favours the player who keeps *sente* (plays so as to make the opponent keep answering) in a major way.

At the stage of filling the neutral points nothing is apparently at stake. However, it is important to see that even then the plays can be classified by *sente* and *gote*. Of those just seen, B and D were *sente* for White (threatened to gain points if not answered), E was *sente* for Black.

8.2 Neutral point or *sente* play?

Any play that creates a cutting point, or simply fills an outside liberty of a chain, may be an attempt to cause mischief. If there is no clear benefit to your opponent, making or defending territory, it is perhaps a trick. This is a practical difficulty. We have the two important distinctions in hand:

- ■ Neutral points versus plays that are worth something.
- ■ *Sente* plays versus *gote* plays.

Is it a *gote* neutral point or a *sente* play of value?

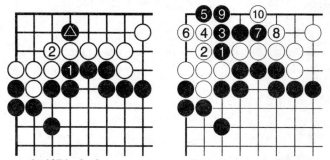

For example, if Black plays to create a cutting point here in White's wall, it is wrong for White to connect (**left**), even though the marked Black stone looks dangerous. If White plays correctly (**right**) the capturing race is hopeless for Black. Playing safe – treating more of your opponent's plays as *sente* than they really are – may seem better than erring in the other direction. But that attitude won't do if you want to come close to being a *dan* player. You cannot rely on your opponent not to try tricks; rely on yourself.

8.3 Is it all over?

The game ends when both players pass in succession.

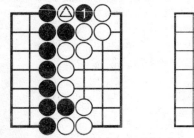

In this position there is a good reason for the game to end with three passes in four plays. Black 1 captures in the *ko*, White says 'pass', Black 3 connects the *ko*, White says 'pass', and Black says 'pass'. With 2, White should neither play inside Black's territory, nor fill her own. Those plays would lose a point. As it is, the game ends with 14 points of territory each, so that if the captives are equal it would be a draw.

8.4 Is it really all over?

The game has finished, both players passing. There may still be:

- Neutral points to play. Some may be surprising, for example captures within *seki* positions (p.212).
- Problem areas of the board, which are not properly finished.
- Plays that one player thinks are *gote* neutral points, but the other player thinks require a reply.

The game is actually over (in competition the clocks would be stopped). There are the following points of protocol to deal with these matters:

- The players fill the neutral points before any hopeless stones are removed or any rearrangement is made for counting.
- Where there are disagreements, and no stronger player to adjudicate, the situations are played out.

It is best to record positions before doing the latter, or to play out on a second board. If this is not practical, continue the game under 'confirmation phase rules' – add an equal number of Black and White stones, any pass being marked by giving the opponent a prisoner. The net score will not change if plays inside territory fail.

8.5 Take up the bodies

Some games do indeed resemble the end of Act V of Hamlet, with large numbers of hopeless dead stones to be removed. If you think questionable stones are still useful, don't say 'pass'. When the game is agreed to be over, it is over. You should concede hopeless stones gracefully.

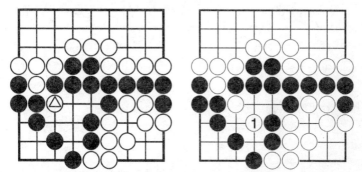

However, you cannot be certain of the status of hopeless-looking stones as 'dead'. This example shows how the marked White stone can play a part in the game. White 1 threatens both a snapback and a cut. In fact, rather than White being hopeless, Black is helpless.

There are two classes of problems apparently hopeless stones can cause:

■ They may assist in break-ins.

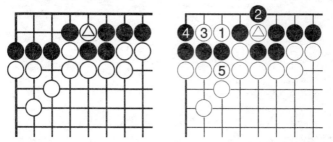

The game isn't over in this part of the board. White plays 1 on the inside, rather than the neutral point 5 on the outside here.

■ They may make life on their own. That includes life by *seki* or *ko*. Some areas, particularly big corners, are a little too large for comfort, and give good chances to the invader.

8.6 Break-in disasters

In fact the two classes of endgame difficulties mentioned in 8.5 are more generally the usual causes of major losses in the endgame (so-called 'swindles'). However caused, and whether occurring in the closing plays or earlier, they make for much frustration in the learner Go player.

This section examines a case in the first category, loss of territory by direct break-in. This can generally be attributed to having too many cutting points. There have been a number of earlier examples.

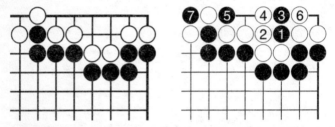

This surprisingly complex example ought to impress you on two grounds: it looks like a completely natural position from a real game (it is), and there seems also nothing reasonable for Black to try. Black can in fact do something with a play at one of the cutting points **(right)**. This is an exercise in visualizing a snapback well ahead of its appearance on the board.

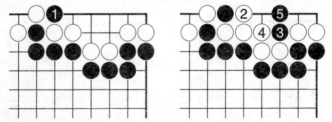

In a real game it would be important not to stop there, but to wonder what else might work. 'If you see a good play, look for a better one' is an old saying, of particular relevance to this sort of position. If Black considers changing the order of plays, what about Black 1 **(left)**? If White captures it Black still has a break-in **(right)**. This sort of position is called 'double *damezumari*', after the Japanese term meaning 'lacking liberties'. It is another case in which chase down of 3.4 can fail, and is at least as hard to see as a snapback.

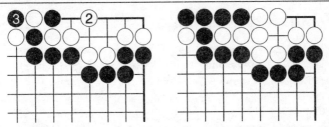

If White reacts to save the corner with 2 **(left)**, Black can capture as before. Now the White territory will amount only to three points at the end of the game **(right)**.

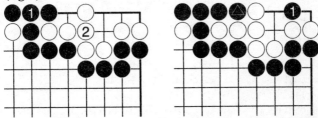

Going into this point in a little more detail reveals another layer to the position. It may look as if White can connect at 2 when Black fills at the neutral point 1 **(left)**, to defend four points. But when Black fills another neutral point outside **(right)**, White has to play inside once more to prevent Black playing inside at 1. White has three points only.

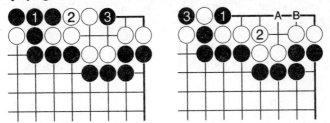

More on this position. **(Left)** White strains to get five points in the corner, but is punished. **(Right)** Yet another try by White. After 3 the corner is already alive (Black A, White B works). But White will have only three points in the corner at the end.

Summing up: The second method is the correct way for Black to carry out this break-in. It leaves White alive in the corner with just three points; the first way shown gives three points and two captives, so is worse for Black.

8.7 Making life inside

In an attempt to make isolated stones live, when that appears unreasonable, the attacker is normally running little risk – perhaps wasting some *ko* threats, or giving away a few points. Such tries are too often speculative. It can be more interesting to take the defender's point of view, and look how to kill the intruders.

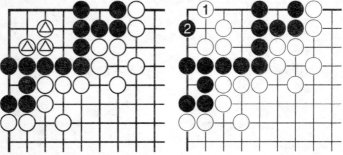

Here Black has two eyes, and must simply stop White making life. This is easy since the marked stones can live only with both the points 1 and 2.

The next example belongs to a class of problems of much greater difficulty, with enough space for the attacker to try a number of tricks, and no definite eye shape for the defender. It comes from 1.5.

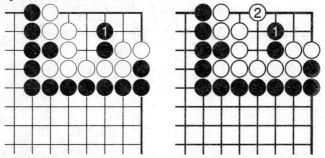

(**Left**) Black can't hope to kill White in this case, but has some prospect of a *seki*. (**Right**) White should try to build an eye, either on the left or in the corner. The principle mentioned in 7.7, that a *seki* doesn't occur between a chain with one eye and a chain with no eye, is a great help in this position. White can stop Black making an eye, so the pressure is now on Black to prevent White completing one.

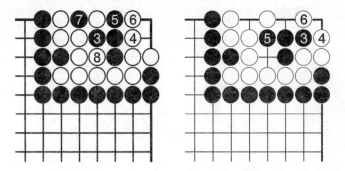

These two continuations show White finishing Black off. There is no *seki* here. In fact 8 in the left-hand diagram is an unnecessary play. But 6 in the right-hand diagram is required (Black at 6 would make a *seki*).

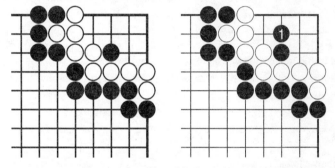

However, small differences matter greatly. In this case Black does make a *seki*.

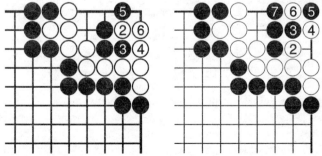

(**Left**) Black succeeds in making a *seki*, in *sente*. (**Right**) White unwisely tries to avoid that result, but a *ko* arises in the corner.

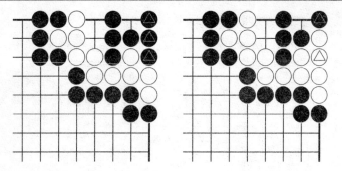

White isn't likely to be happy with this *ko*, and its possible outcomes.
(Left) If Black wins the two *kos* in sequence in the corner, and connects,
the capturing race in the corner is over, and White has lost. **(Right)** White
connects the second of the *kos*. The resulting position is a postponed or ten
thousand year *ko* (7.6). But Black may well fight this as a picnic *ko*. This
was White's corner, initially. Towards the end of the game Black may find
it profitable to start the *ko*. Here picnic actually translates 'cherry-blossom
viewing', a Japanese custom involving open-air food and alcohol; so the
connotation is 'carefree'.

These examples aren't chosen for their strange properties. They illustrate
difficulties with big corners, which are seen in real games.

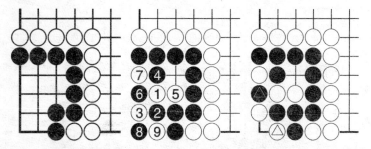

Here is another one, not uncommon in beginners' games. The result of
White's invasion is a double *ko*. Black will always respond to a *ko* capture
by White, such as 9, by another *ko* capture **(right)**. It is Black who can live
here, and White who has no chance to, so that Black is alive under the
ruling in 7.6. The White stones will be taken off at the end of the game, but
for the time being White has unlimited *ko* threats.

8.8 Cutting point disasters

It may seem to the reader who has played a few games of Go that the examples given so far in this chapter are of much more sophisticated ways of losing than are seen in most games. Some of the usual troubles were shown in 3.4 and 3.5. In fact the advantage experienced players have over the novice in the endgame is more to do with being able to bring to bear all the standard tactical skills, than any special insights.

There is more to cutting points than just the possibility of cutting at them, a topic seen already in many places.

Peeping

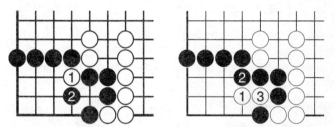

In this position cutting at the cutting point is a failure (**left**). But peeping next to it means that White will cut at 2 or at 3 (**right**).

Threatening snapback

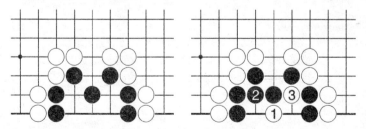

Black seems safe, perhaps. But when White plays at the centre there is no time to defend on both sides. White 1 sets up two possible snapbacks.

It is more amusing when this happens to someone else.

8.9 More danger on the edge

There is a common way of starting a *ko* fight with a play on the second line, which can prove very expensive until you learn it.

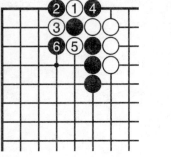

When there is a cutting point at 5 as in the left-hand diagram, Black must concede a little. (**Left**) Playing at 2 here is careless. White cuts and a serious *ko* arises. Black could lose heavily. (**Right**) Black must run back one further, and is then quite safe.

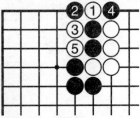

This position, with a Black cutting point on the third line, is very similar, and just as painful. Black concedes a little for safety (**right**).

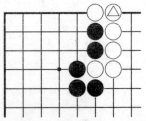
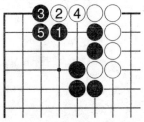

When White has the extra marked stone, the situation is one in which many players come to grief, not knowing how much to concede. Jumping back (**right**) stops White and keeps most of the corner.

8.10 The routine plays

This chapter has quite deliberately been structured so that the most common problems for those learning the game are mentioned first, and the endgame knowledge routinely assumed by strong players comes last of all.

To present some of that body of information, we use the normal shorthand. This consists of:

■ Description of plays (means introduction of the Japanese term *hane*, pronounced 'hah-nay').

■ Classification of plays as *sente* and *gote*.

■ Counting of plays, properly broken down.

We explain these matters first. The common plays tend to be those on the edge, and in fact on the first and second lines. The word *hane*, which has come into general Go usage, means a play 'round the end' of the opponent.

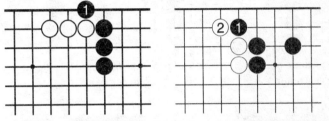

You should recognize by now that this is the most common way to reduce the opponent's territory, when it isn't possible to jump right in. No recognized English term translates *hane*.

The standard classification of plays is by the situation, in which either player may play first: *sente* for Black and for White, also called 'double *sente*'; *sente* for one player but *gote* for the other; and 'double *gote*', that is, losing the initiative for either player. The four kinds, including *sente* for Black and *sente* for White as two, are to be thought of quite differently.

Counting of plays matters most for double *gote* plays. In choosing amongst those, one should play them in order of decreasing value. Two plays of exactly the same value should go one to each player; but with accurate counting you can make exchanges of *gote* plays that favour you slightly. Over a long endgame the gain may be substantial.

Giving up a play to prevent your opponent's *sente* play can be skilful. The theory of when to do this requires too much detail for this book.

First line *hane*-connect plays

Many examples have occurred already.

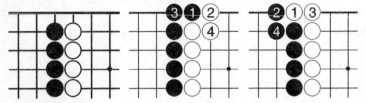

A double *sente* play worth four points. Playing here makes an absolute difference of four points in the score. It is a very urgent play. The four points should be visible.

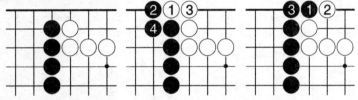

This is three points *sente* for White. White will expect to be able to play here and retain the initiative. **(Right)** *Gote* for Black.

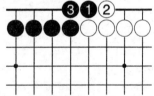

Two point double *gote*. This is a small play. It will only be taken by one or other player when the game is close to finishing.

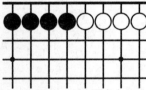

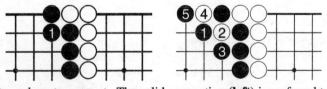

A note on how to connect. The solid connection **(left)** is preferred to the hanging connection **(right)**, in order not to leave *ko* threats at 2, and 4. But the hanging connection often has some advantages, too; particularly for making eye shape. They can outweigh the *ko* threats.

Second line *hane*-connect plays

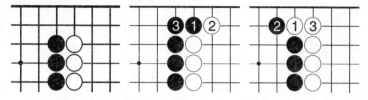

This is a double *gote* play worth six points plus. In the case shown the plus is quite large – four points on each side, making the total value 14 points.

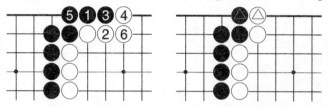

This shows the extra four points from Black's point of view, taking into account what was said in 8.9, with the baseline shown (**right**).

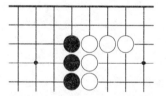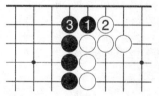

The same reasoning applies to this position, where Black's *hane*-connect doesn't have a *sente* follow-up, to give it a value of 10 points.

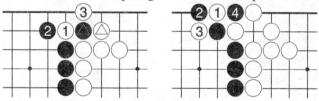

The same value applies to this position, the exchange of the triangled stones not changing matters greatly. But in fact, if Black is determined to make a *ko* on the edge (**right**), White has more at risk than in the comparable position seen before (first example on p.138).

8.11 Area counting

A different counting method, called area counting, can be used at the end of a game of Go. It differs from the method shown in this book, called territory counting; but the difference of the scores in the game is usually changed by one point, or is unchanged. In area counting:

- The total area controlled by your stones, occupied by your stones or surrounded as empty points, is your score.
- No points are given for captives.

Assume:

- An even game (i.e. the board started empty).
- No *seki* positions on the board.
- All the possible *gote* neutral points were filled alternately, and the *sente* neutral points were answered, before the game ended with its only two passes.

Then it is easy to work out the relation between 'territory' and 'area' scores. The margin in the game is the same under the two systems if White played last, and if Black played last it is changed by one in favour of Black under the 'area' rules. Unless the game is very close, so that the one point of area for filling the final neutral point matters, or there is a complication with *seki*, you can play the same way under the two systems. The rule sets for Go don't substantially affect the skills of the Go player (see Appendix).

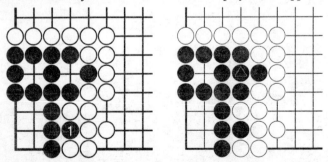

A useful exercise to ponder, to understand area rules: it may be better to play a neutral point 1 (**left**), then later connect the half-point *ko* (**right**).

Area counting is generally used in China. Your Chinese opponent is likely to return your prisoners to your bowl, since there is no need to keep them for scoring. Sometimes people refer loosely to 'the Chinese rules'.

8.12 Problems

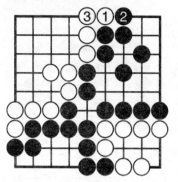
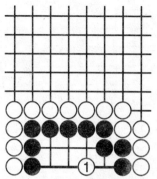

1. (Left) Is this game over? Should Black pass now?

2. (Right) How should Black answer?

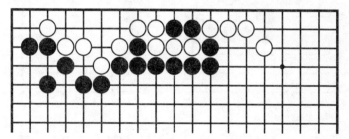

3. White to play.

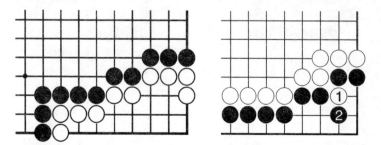

4. (Left) Black to play. (A real position from one of my games.)

5. (Right) White has found a good move. What now?

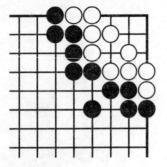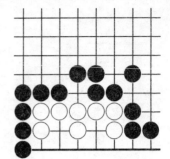

6,7. Black to play.

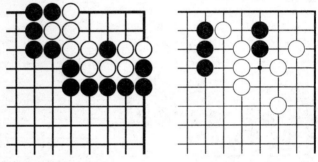

8,9. Black to play.

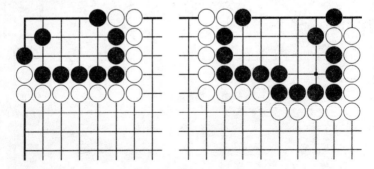

10,11. Black to play. In both cases Black has a cutting point on the second line. Is a further play inside called for?

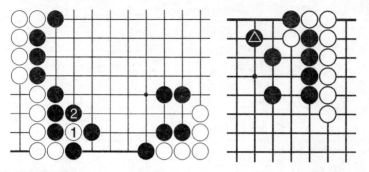

12. (Left) White has a way to break in, starting with the sacrifice 1.

13. (Right) White to play. Black has defended well against a break-in, with the marked stone. How does White continue from here?

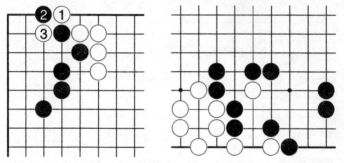

14. (Left) What is White trying here?

15. (Right) Since Black has been careless, White has something unusual to try. (Observed on the Internet.)

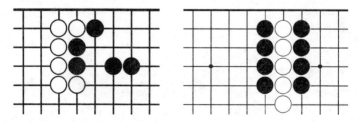

16. (Left) White has something interesting to play.

17. (Right) White can stir up some mischief here.

8.13 Solutions

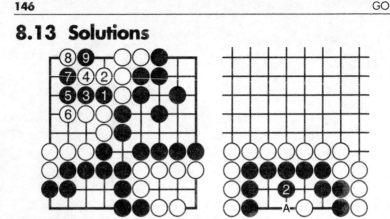

1. (Left) White loses when Black cuts. **2. (Right)** White has nothing good here. Black plays 2. Black at A instead might turn into a *seki* or *ko*.

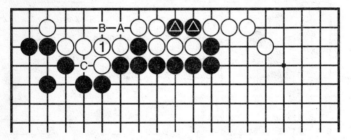

3. Because of the two marked stones Black has a way to break in with A, which White answers at B for a *ko*. White at 1 is the best way to defend, since White will need to play here anyway after Black C.

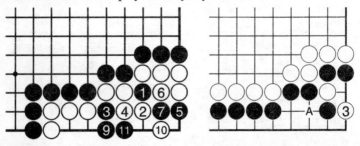

4. (Left) White 8 at 1. Black manages to break in by 'double *damezumari*'.
5. (Right) White 3 is best. It uses a snapback to capture the two Black stones, and threatens to play next at A.

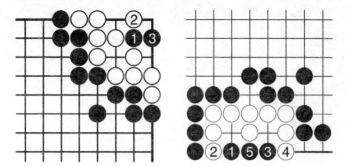

6,7. In both cases Black can make a *seki*.

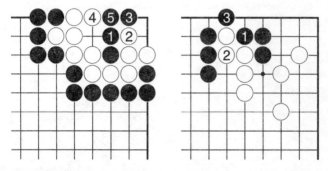

8. (Left) When Black plays 1, the best White can get is a ten thousand year *ko* (7.6). **9. (Right)** Black connects out easily with 1.

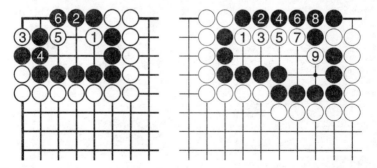

10. (Left) Black needs no play inside here. Neither White 1, 3, and 5, nor any other combination of plays, give Black any problems. **11. (Right)** In this case Black must add something. White can break in by simple means.

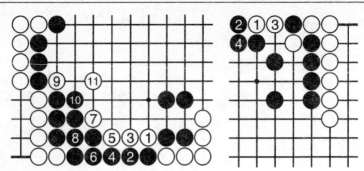

12. (Left) White can in fact capture Black on a big scale, if it gets as far as 11, a defective net but highly effective when Black tries to get out.

13. (Right) White's best *sente* plays in this position.

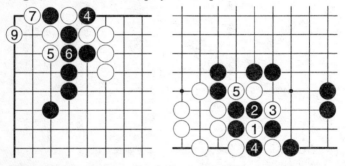

14. (Left) White is aiming to live in the corner if Black 8 is the connection. So Black will start a *ko* instead, with 8 cutting below 7. **15. (Right)** Black forgot to play at 1, the key point. White makes a *ko*.

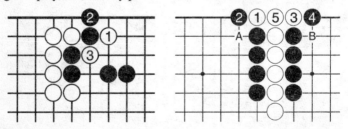

16. (Left) The clamp at 1 breaks up more Black territory than a play on the first line. **17. (Right)** Black has problems here, caused by the two cutting points at A and B. Better for Black is to answer 1 by playing 2 at 3, then jump back as on p.138 when White plays 3 at 5.

9 | CORNERS AND SIDES

9.1 The 4–4 point

A game of Go almost invariably starts in the corners of the board, plays on the sides or in the centre being experiments. In recent times the most common way to occupy a corner has been with a play on the 4–4 point.

In classical Go the dominant opening play in the corner was the 3–4 point. But in contemporary Go at the top level, players occupy the corner at the 4–4 point perhaps 70 per cent of the time.

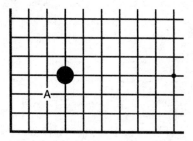

The feature of the 4–4 point that first requires comment is the possibility of 3–3 invasion, already shown in 2.4. White can play at A and live. But then with correct play Black will build a strong wall on the outside.

The popularity of the 4–4 point play with professional players shows that it is a sound strategy. In a way characteristic of Go, it is an indirect play. Black will gain in the corner or on the outside, depending on what White does.

The 4–4 point is also used for handicaps. In a handicap game White hopes, perhaps, that an invasion at the 3–3 point will leave Black without adequate compensation on the outside for the loss of points in the corner. Black will learn to use the 4–4 point to control the play in this corner of the board, and the proper way to exploit influence on the side of the board and in the centre.

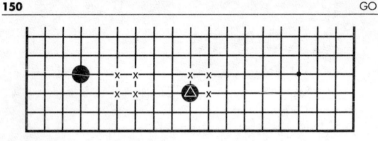

In adding to the 4–4 point an extra stone, such as the marked extension to the 10–3 point, Black has to have thought ahead to the 3–3 invasion. The points marked with 'x' work well, and the intermediate points generally don't.

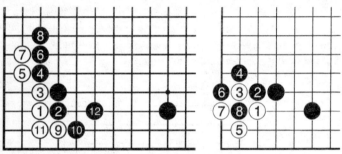

With a distant extension, Black intends to block on the right of the invasion, if it comes, making a wall that works well with the stone already played **(left)**. The stones closer to the corner are played with the intention of blocking on the other side **(right)**. Then White has a harder struggle to live – in the case shown, a *ko*.

There is another possibility for Black to consider when White invades.

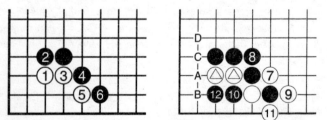

Black 6 is less dangerous than it may look. On the right Black has taken the corner back (White is captured after White A, Black B, White C, Black D).

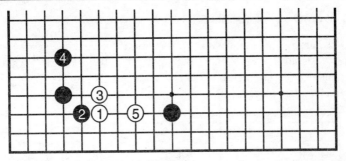

If White chooses to play an approach move to the corner as shown here, Black can get a good development with the diagonal attachment 1. The three Black stones in the corner are working much better than White's three on the side.

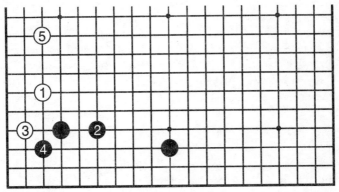

It is more reasonable for White to play the approach move from the other side, and make a stable group on the left. Black 4 is the correct play.

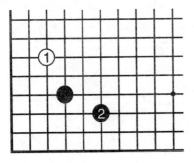

When White plays the approach move and Black has no other stone in place in this part of the board, Black 2 (**left**) is a good response. The one-point jump above is also normally good, but may lead to problems if White is strong on the lower side.

9.2 The 3–4 point

Plays at the 3–4 point make up almost all the other opening corner moves in professional Go. The residue, perhaps 2 per cent, goes to the 3–3 and 5–3 points. The 5–4 point (part of classical Go), the 5–5, 6–3 and 6–4 points are exotic when played.

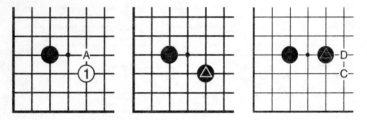

Each opening corner play has its own characteristics. For the 3–4 point they are stability, and an orientation towards territory. White makes an approach move play near the corner with 1 or A. If not, Black will enclose it with another play. **(Centre)** This knight's move enclosure is justly popular, especially with amateur players. It takes a firm hold of the corner. **(Right)** Other enclosures are also used. Black adds the marked stone, or one at C or D. These enclosures are intermediate in their control of the corner. They are not as easy to invade as the 4–4 point, but not as tight on territory as the knight's move enclosure.

The other characteristic of the 3–4 point that deserves comment is that it is asymmetric, where the 4–4 point is symmetric.

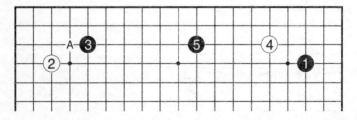

Here is one of the teachings of the traditional masters. White normally plays 2 at A, not as shown. The reason is that Black 5 works very well in relation to Black 1 and Black 3. Black 5 is a typical *pincer* move, and here it is considered ideal for Black.

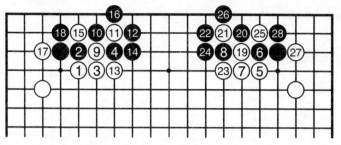

Another piece of wisdom of this kind: Black should not allow this to happen. White makes the most of the opening mentioned on p.63. Black is doing badly because the strong stones 12 and 14 are too close to 22 and 24. White gains more on the outside.

Identifiable mistakes, such as those pointed out in the last two diagrams, are not very common at the stage of occupying corners and playing approach moves. When there are a few more stones on the board it becomes harder to find the best moves, because *you have to take into account what has already been played*. This can count as the basic slogan of Go strategy.

The pincer shown on the previous page is a good all-round answer when your opponent plays the low (5–3) approach to your 3–4 point.

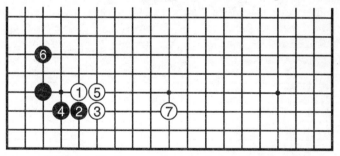

In the case of the high (5–4) approach to the 3–4 point, this typical opening can be recommended. After White plays 7 there is no reason for Black to continue in this part of the board. Black 2 has the plan of taking the corner, and the opening proceeds peacefully. White establishes a good position on the side, but has less solid territory than Black has surrounded in the corner.

Black ends with *sente* here – Black can choose where to play next on the board. The initiative is important throughout the game.

9.3 Home-made openings

If your opponent hasn't read this book, or any other literature on Go, you may be faced with quite different corner openings.

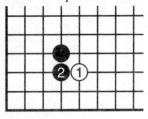 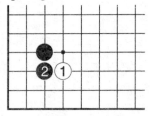

Approach moves that come too close are easily dealt with, as here.

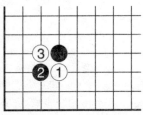 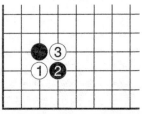

Some aggressive players will play even closer, with the sole intention of making a cross-cut (4.2) and starting a fight. You can avoid that by playing 2 at 3 in both these diagrams (see 2.4 about this). In general, contact plays such as White makes here don't lead to advantage. *Answer contact plays.* This advice is the complement to *don't play too close* yourself.

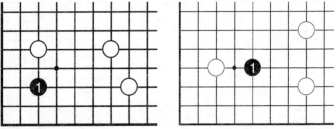

Perhaps harder to deal with is the opponent who makes strange, irregular enclosures like these. You will learn more by trying to invade them than by letting the corner fall into White's hands on a large scale. In both of these cases Black tries an invasion after three stones have been played. **(Left)** It will be hard for White to kill this 3–3 invasion. **(Right)** Here Black may run away, or live in the area.

9.4 The evolution of openings

The corner openings in Go have been studied in great depth.

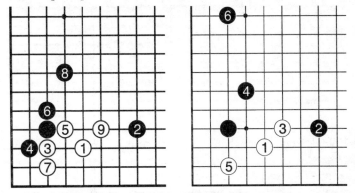

Here is an example. The sequence on the left is considered obsolete, and has been replaced by the one on the right. Advantages are:

- ■ White has avoided exchanges that strengthen Black.
- ■ Black on the left can resist by playing 6 at 7.
- ■ White finishes with *sente*.

Experience shows that White cannot be attacked strongly.

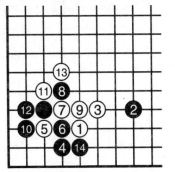
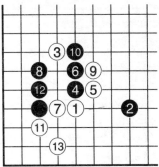

(**Left**) Experiments continue, such as this one.

(**Right**) The comparable standard sequence for the high approach took a generation to develop.

The good news is that you need not worry initially about studying these openings. Wait until you are about 4 *kyu* (average club player).

9.5 Wedging on the side

How best to deal with the 4–4 point?

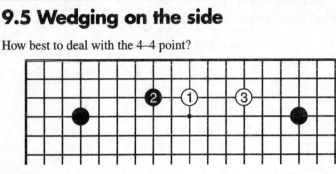

One idea is to play at a safe distance, aiming to establish a group before invading the corner or playing an approach move. The *wedge* play White 1 here has the advantage that White can spread out and play a two-point extension (4.5) on one side or the other.

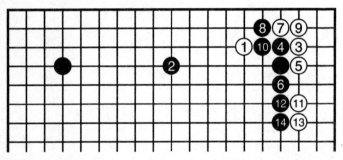

If White plays an approach move more directly, Black may pincer. The sequence in the right-hand corner is standard, but Black's resulting position on the side is very good.

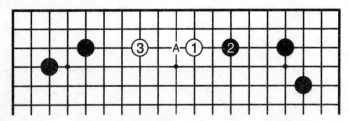

The wedge is useful in other ways. Here White breaks up Black's side. White 1 at A would also function as a wedge. But then Black would move 2 one point to the left too, for a more efficient extension.

9.6 Extending the proper distance

Since the Go stones don't move, it is a worse mistake to crowd them too close together, than to spread them too far apart. You can come back and defend where you are weak – where you are stronger than necessary there is nothing to be done.

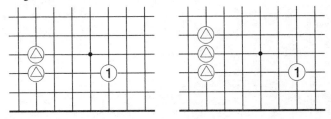

Important examples for that principle are the standard lengths of extension from walls. *From a two-stone wall extend three spaces* (**left**). *From a three-stone wall extend four spaces* (**right**). Anything less is too narrow.

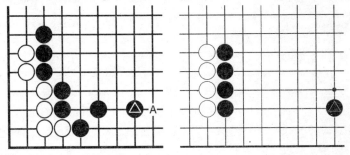

Looking back at 9.1, some of the comments there can be added to. In the left-hand diagram the marked Black stone would definitely be too close to the Black wall; even at A it would be too close. If one line further away is considered correct, perhaps the Black wall ought to be thought of as equivalent to the four-stone wall in the right-hand diagram. *From a four-stone wall extend five* is a good guess. In a game you have to examine possible invasion sequences, but the point is to make proper use of your existing strength.

The trouble with playing your stones too close together is that you may lose without realizing what is happening. Losses in efficiency are small mistakes, but they mount up over the course of a game. Try reading section 2.3 again now.

9.7 Proper extensions from enclosures

The standard length of extensions from enclosures is greater than would be expected by trying to regard them as walls. The principle here is that enclosures already have adequate eye space. As the saying goes, 'Walls may have ears, but they have no eyes.'

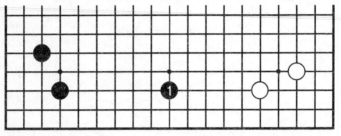

Black should extend as far as 1 here. Anything less is timid.

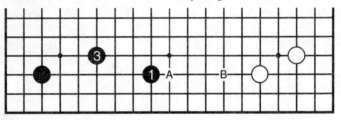

The 3–3 point functions like an enclosure made with one play. The tent formation made here with 1 and 3 is very good – one of the few ways of building a territory with just three plays. Black could also play A, then B, to make a larger and looser framework.

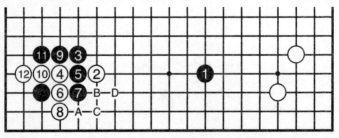

Something very different – an imaginative sacrifice variation from a professional game. The 'open skirt' at the left is serious. But Black has anticipated White A up to Black D. Black 1 is nicely positioned.

9.8 Frameworks built from enclosures

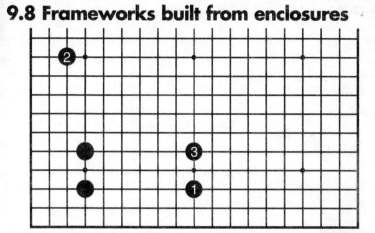

Enclosures should be developed on the grand scale. First playing an extension on the front (Black 1), then one to the side (Black 2), then building a box shape in the centre (Black 3), Black claims over 50 points of territory.

White can still invade this area, or reduce it from outside, but such a framework promises Black a sustained initiative if White plays in this quarter of the board.

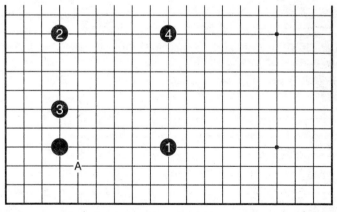

For comparison, here is a framework built around a 4–4 point. White should invade here before Black secures the corner with a further play at A. The good plays for developing frameworks tend to be much more obvious than the ways to counter them.

9.9 Problems, discussion

It is harder to give strategic problems with clear-cut solutions.

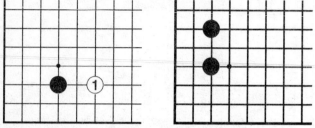

Two unorthodox positions. **1. (Left)** What should Black do now?
2. (Right) What should White do in this corner?

Discussion

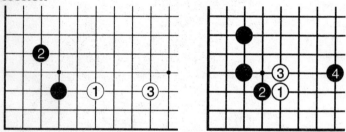

1. (Left) If Black encloses the corner, and White extends, Black has a good result.

2. (Right) White must not approach as close as this. Black can attack strongly.

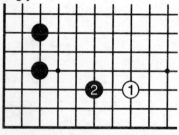 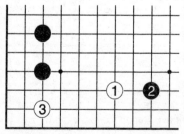

(Left) It is probably better not to play here immediately, and to play at a safe distance. Here White 1 allows Black an enclosure, but is safe.
(Right) Even this is too close – Black attacks with 2, White 3 is too low.

10 | FULL BOARD OPENINGS

10.1 Openings on the full board

The opening in Go is studied on two levels. The corner openings have been mentioned in Chapter 9. These are sequences that may come to a definite end, or result in fights that spill out all over the board. They are repeated in game after game, and can be learned; though that will do you little good unless you understand their constituent plays, how to fit them into the rest of the board position, and how they should be modified in differing circumstances.

The higher level of opening theory concerns the board as a whole, not broken up into four corners. It is on a plane of difficulty that sets it apart. Even considering just the good plays, the global openings seem to branch out twice as fast as the local sequences. The evidence is that in typical opening positions on the full board, there may be four or five respectable choices. Even in the most complex corner openings a choice of three good variations at any given juncture is a little unusual. In the past it has been considered that there is simply not enough material from top level games to study the openings in depth, in what might seem the obvious fashion. Instead, players have concentrated on the general principles, and research that deliberately leads the game onto unfamiliar ground.

Modern professional players are moving away from that traditional and artistic slant on the openings – trying to 'make it afresh' each game – to an apparently more scientific approach. Recent research undertaken by the Korean pros appears to be more systematic than anything seen in the past.

Concentration on the openings is often seen as a way of correcting the bad habit of self-taught players of relying too much on their fighting skill. In one of the most interesting and hopeful developments in international Go, Chinese and Korean players have seen improved opening theory as a way of carrying the battle to the Japanese, long undisputed leaders as the Go-playing nation.

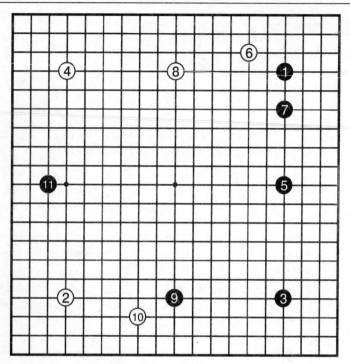

Example 1: 'Three Stars'

The name refers to the three star points on the right-hand side occupied by Black with plays 1, 3 and 5. This opening can lead to a contest of frameworks in the centre, and then heavy fighting.

The first four plays each occupy one of the empty corners. This is usual, since the corners are the most important parts of the board. With 5, Black sketches out a formation on the right-hand side on a large scale. To counter Black's expansion White plays an approach move with 6. With the wedge play at 11 Black prevents White from making a 'three stars' formation on the left.

This opening is typical of modern pro play – but isn't very easy to understand. Nothing about territory has been settled yet, meaning many issues remain. The players have even avoided any contact between stones, up to this point. Each of the four corners may still be invaded at the 3–3 point. If Black invades behind 2, White has to remember the third diagram on p.157.

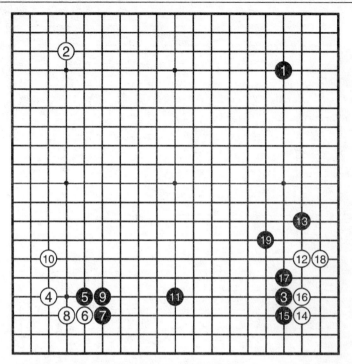

Example 2: 'Two Stars'

In this case White plays differently on the left-hand side. Black takes note of the position of White 4 to play an approach move 5 that combines well with the 4–4 point in the lower right. The opening in the lower left corner is the one from p.153, except that Black 11 is played on the fourth line. This choice means White finds it harder to reduce the framework that appears on the lower side. In this position it is consistent for Black to play 15 rather than 16, when White invades with 14.

At the end of the plays shown, White has to pay attention to how to develop the top left corner of the board. Simply enclosing the top left corner allows Black to extend to the centre of the top side. White so far has two secure corners, so can consider extending there first. Conventional wisdom says the enclosure play is worth more points than any play on the side, but Black is in no hurry to approach the top left corner. The White stone at 10 is very solid, meaning Black can achieve little on the left side.

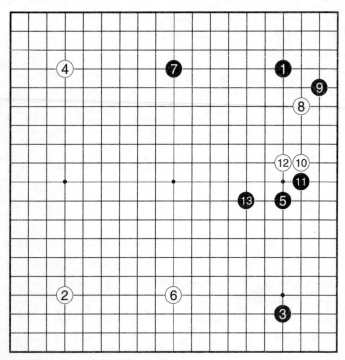

Example 3: 'The Chinese Style'

In the 1970s a fresh opening idea became highly fashionable. Black 5 was played, not as an enclosure in the lower right corner, but as an extension on the side, one line below the star point. The history is complicated, but the name 'Chinese Style' has stuck, with considerable justification.

The variation shown has White plunging into the right side very early on in the game. Black attacks, with the intention of building up territory in the top right and lower right corners. For the present, White has to concentrate on defending the stones 8, 10, and 12. They have become a weak group: they don't have enough space for two eyes, so must run out into the centre.

Between strong players the game would remain balanced, with White stabilizing the group quite soon and then considering developing the left side or invading Black's corners. But the Chinese is a rapid pattern, often bowling over the inexperienced player as White.

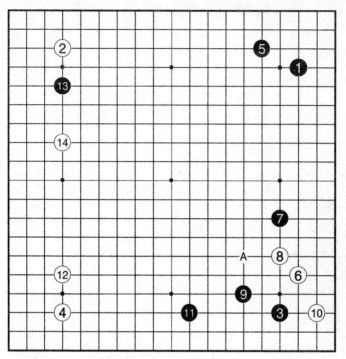

Example 4: 'The Enclosure Opening'

This is the only one of our examples that doesn't have Black starting at the 4–4 point. In the 1950s and 1960s the 3–4 point was the routine play. The elements of the opening were all discussed in Chapter 9. The small adjustment in the corner opening from 9.4 in the lower right, with 11 moved one line to the right, takes into account the way a White play at A would affect both sides.

Going back, Black's pincer 7 is designed to make the most of the enclosure in the top right corner. White has a large choice in answering it. But the way shown has the definite virtue of making White hard to attack. Compare with Example 3, where White's group is afloat in the middle.

Summary

These openings are representative, but the range of possible strategies is enormous.

11 | THE MIDDLEGAME

11.1 The elements

The middlegame tends to be long – usually beginning by move 40 and continuing for a hundred plays or more – and complex, as unexpected situations result from invasions and attacks. It is hard to keep a grip on the whole position. Here are the ideas we shall work with, in this chapter.

Weak groups, frameworks and thickness

Weak groups are stones that have trouble finding space for two eyes. Frameworks are potential territories that may still be invaded. Thickness means a position with outside influence and free from obvious weaknesses such as undefended cutting points.

Influence, direction, strategic mistakes

Influence is an important idea in Go. For example, in the game in Chapter 6 the group White makes in the top left corner has influence, an effect on the game out of all proportion to the rather small number of points of territory in it. In 2.3 the influence of walls was considered.

However, the general concept of 'influence' is too vague. Normally groups of stones have only a short-range effect on the game (ladders along their path, and *kos*, provide exceptions). But close together weak groups, frameworks and thickness interact in particular ways: influence works along channels that can be identified, providing natural *directions of play*. The logic of Go is to follow them. Not to do so can be a strategic mistake. Can a game with such freedom of choice be so constrained? You perhaps think that tactical considerations can override strategy. In time you may decide that it is easier to go with the flow. The main points are brought together in the box opposite, the rest of the chapter being full of examples.

Strategic ideas on influence

Frameworks and thickness are different kinds of influence – two extreme cases. Weak groups require defence, so they are acted upon by influence more than they influence the game.

- Weak groups are like *animals* – mobile, requiring constant attention, the dynamic part of Go.
- Frameworks are *vegetable* – they grow organically, are easily damaged.
- Thickness is *mineral* – diamond-like, hard and must be put to proper use, displayed in the best light.

Frameworks are half-made territory. The object is to complete the territory, or to take control of the game if the opponent invades. It is good to strengthen and develop frameworks on their edges, and bad to chase the opponent into them.

Thickness is outward-facing influence that has no defects and so needs no improvement. It is good to lead fighting towards your thickness. It is bad to attempt to make relatively small amounts of territory near your thickness, early in the game.

Key directions – the conclusions

In *running fights*, jump out into the centre to avoid being shut in, look for *base plays* that build eyes for both.

Splitting attacks, with two weak groups belonging to one player attacked at the same time, are very telling.

Take territory while attacking: build up a framework by attacking the opponent's weak group.

Push towards thickness: encourage your opponent into defending where your thickness is.

Focal points: occupy points that build your framework while diminishing your opponent's one. *Getting shut in* is a bad idea.

Invasions backed up by thickness have a better chance of success.

Much thickness in one place makes it a *low priority area*.

11.2 Weak groups together

We shall now consider possible combinations in pairs of the three fundamentals from 11.1 in turn, on the assumption that they occur close on the board. There are enough basic remarks to make to put together a survey of middlegame possibilities

Two weak groups, of opposite colours

This is the situation called a *running fight*, as both weak groups try to escape to the centre.

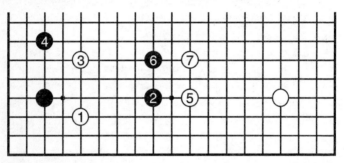

A 'pincer-counterpincer' opening, in which White deliberately starts a running fight on the side, to make the most of the 4–4 point in the right-hand corner. White now has a framework based on it.

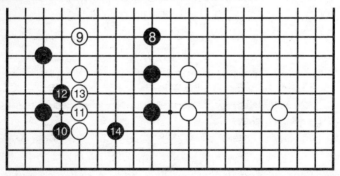

The next plays in this running fight are typical. Both players jump out, and then Black concentrates on White's eye space. After 10 and 12 to the left, Black plays the key point at 14. Either player would gain an advantage, at least one eye, by making a 'base' at this point.

Two weak groups, same colour

It is very dangerous to have two of your weak groups in the same part of the board. Here is an example of what may happen – a *splitting attack*.

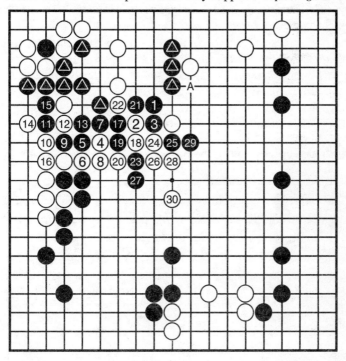

Another position from one of my teaching games. Black hadn't played very well on the left side, allowing the top left to become weak (marked stones). White then went after the Black stones in the middle of the upper side (also marked). But Black 1 here is the major error. Black should play something like A, to develop away from the top left. Trying to connect, and failing as here, is much worse. Black lost the top left, which can't form two eyes, and resigned.

Good players take into account the need not to be attacked like this very early on (before invading and making the second group, for example). Such planning is characteristic from the stronger amateur levels. So it is unusual to find such illustrations of the splitting attack idea in high-class games.

11.3 A weak group near a framework

Weak group near a framework, colours opposite

Your opponent's weak group near your framework should be attacked so as to build up the framework. There was an example for this on p.57.

What you should not do is drive the weak group into your framework in order to try to kill it. That is confusion – you are treating your framework on the assumption that it is thickness. For every time you succeed there will be several in which the group lives all over your potential territory. This good advice has never yet had any effect on a certain class of aggressive players. (The phenomenon is so distasteful no example is given.)

Weak group near a framework of the same colour

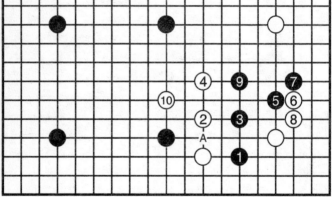

Black invades at 1. This is an example of incorrect strategy. White starts a running fight. While Black is paying attention to the right-hand corner, White finds it easy to broach the Black framework with 10. Now Black needs to strengthen the lower side. A Black attack on the lower right corner is unlikely to recoup as many points as have been lost in the centre.

This whole approach is clumsy on Black's part. Black 1 would have been much better at 2, or A, to develop the large framework on the left further. Black has made precisely the mistake of confusing framework with thickness, applying the pattern of 11.6 which is wrong here. There is a point of principle involved, part of the commonsense of Go.

11.4 A weak group near thickness

We can assume opposite colours; your own group will not be weak near
your thickness, in a way that matters for strategy.

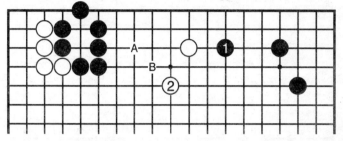

The principle '*push towards thickness*' is illustrated. White moves out with
2, rather than A or even B, extending towards the thick Black group. This
is a typical passage of attack and defence.

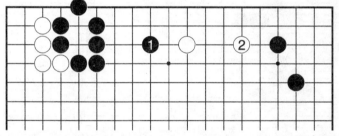

This direction counts as absurd. Black picks up only half a dozen points
with 1. And it is harder to go on attacking White, who has settled right in
front of Black's enclosure.

People go as far as to say 'don't make territory next to your thickness'. You
can take that as meaning that Black will deserve some points as endgame
profit. They should be discounted now.

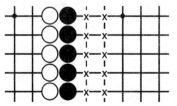

It is consistent with p.19 to visualize this band of future points here.

11.5 Framework by framework

Framework by framework, opposite colours

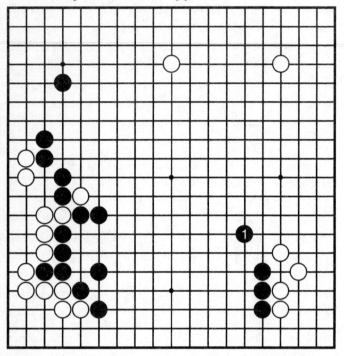

This example is taken from one of my games in the 1998 British Championship, second stage (Challenger's League). Black (David Ward 3 *dan*) has staked everything on a huge framework. Black 1 is at just the right pivotal point to enlarge Black's future potential, while trimming what White can make on the right side. White would have been glad to have played there. Such focal points are typical where frameworks meet.

Framework by framework, same colour

If you are lucky enough to have two frameworks, a play that joins them into one larger framework is likely to be very important. Preventing your opponent from doing this is a very good reason to avoid being shut in.

11.6 Framework next to thickness

The case that matters here is opposite colours. My thickness next to your framework should set the scene for me to invade deeply.

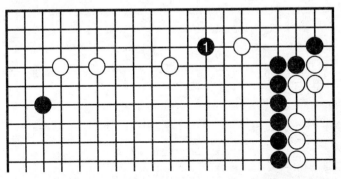

This sort of invasion is one that might happen on the upper side, later on in a game that had started with the opening on p.162. White has invaded quite deeply on the right side, and lived there. In return Black invades the extension White made on the top side, backed up by the 'thickness' formed, i.e. the wall. Since that extension is more loosely connected than the two-point extension of 4.5, White should anticipate this.

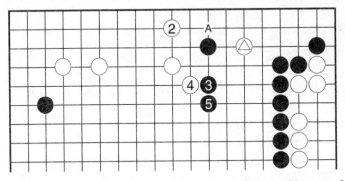

A possible continuation. White avoids starting a fight in this part of the board, where Black is strong. Instead White concedes a calculated amount of territory. The marked White stone is sacrificed. If White later plays at A, it will be found still to have some life in it. If rather than invading with 1 Black had played, say, at 3, allowing White to defend at 1, the thick Black wall would not have been put to good use.

11.7 Thickness near thickness

Thickness near thickness, opposite colours

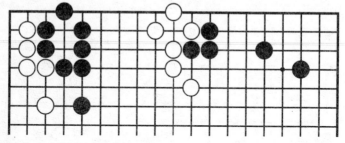

There is not much to say about such situations, except that there are probably no interesting plays in areas where both sides are thick.

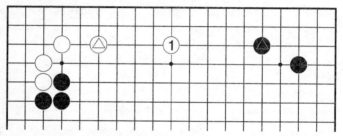

This idea extends to areas where both sides are merely solid. White 1 here is a very dull play, since both marked stones belong to stable groups.

Thickness near thickness of the same colour

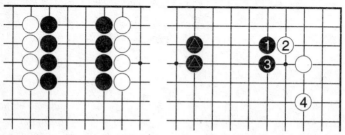

Positions like that on the left violate everything said in 9.6. They are seriously overconcentrated. **(Right)** White plays to make 1 and 3 overlap with the marked stones. See also the example at the top of p.153.

12 | THE GO FINISHING SCHOOL

If you have read this far, you will be familiar with all the components of Go. If you also play regularly, you should make progress. There may come a point when you ask yourself 'How do I improve further?' This chapter offers some suggestions.

In brief

Here is my potted Go course:

  3 Don't let your groups become shut in!
  2 Connect!
  1 Fight!

Of these, 2 is more important than 3; and 1 is more important than 2. You may have to be cut on occasion. But make sure that it is for the sake of fighting, that is, resisting your opponent's plan.

12.1 Ahead and behind

Before turning the page, consider which way you'd play as Black here.

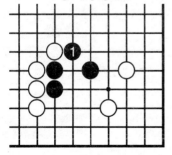 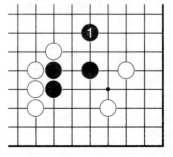

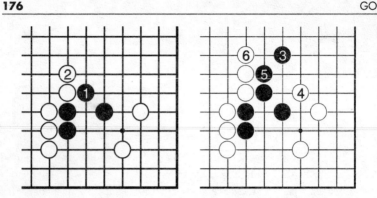

You may well think that by playing Black 1 this way, you'd be making a stronger shape. But by the end of the right-hand diagram Black's attempt to get ahead of White isn't so impressive. Black started too slowly.

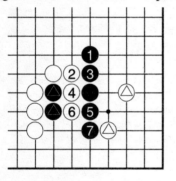

Perhaps the one-point jump out requires a little more vision. It is faster, but is it secure?

White should not try to cut off and capture the two marked Black stones. Black 5 here is admirably relaxed. White's enclosure has been weakened. White had a chance to attack the whole group, but now it is gone.

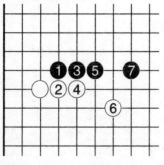

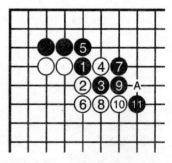

In these sequences the players add stones, so as not to fall behind. **(Left)** Black cannot afford to let White play at 5 or 7. **(Right)** Black 1 and 3 are good, but 11 might provoke White to cut at A.

12.2 Blocking off

You may need to be as tactically acute to block off as for an escape.

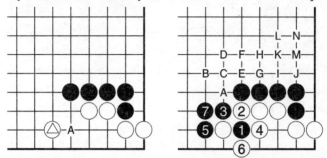

Here White has come out too far. The marked stone would be better at A. Black sacrifices 1 (**right**) to seal off the lower side. Black avoids a hanging connection and annoying peeps by playing at 7. A loose ladder (White at A to Black at N) defends the cut, as an alternative to the ladder north-west.

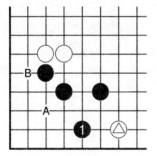

White's marked stone is a typical 'submarine attack' from handicap Go. White's eyes are firmly fixed on a later invasion at A, and then B or 1. Black at 1 solves the immediate problem of blocking off. It is not too close to the White stone, and now if White is at A, Black at B works.

12.3 Mistakes you didn't know you made

One way to improve is to be more observant and self-critical about your plays, even or especially at times when the need to be careful isn't so obvious. Mistakes needn't be catastrophic to pull your level down. It is normal for a game between amateurs to contain many mistakes worth one or two points. They do add up. In Go at large handicaps the player with the White stones is usually able to narrow the margin gradually through the whole game. It is a good idea to start to notice some of the names of common mistakes.

Playing too close

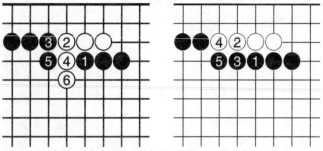

'Squeezing out the toothpaste' – this is deliberately chosen as an extreme case. But mistakes similar to Black's play on the left are often seen. The intention is no doubt to attack, but the right-hand diagram represents sanity.

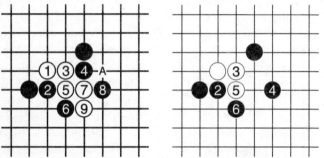

'Failing ladder' – here **(left)** Black 4 is too close. It would be better at A, or even better as on the right, where White is starting to have problems.

Spot the snapback

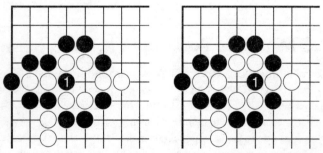

Well, would you here? From a game in which my opponent didn't.

Room for improvement: find a better play than 1

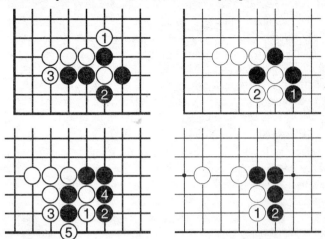

Problems **1, 2, 3, 4** are about the second line. Solutions p.181.

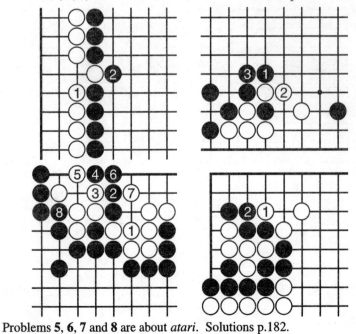

Problems **5, 6, 7** and **8** are about *atari*. Solutions p.182.

12.4 Reading power

Go players commonly complain that the reason they lose games is (solely)
lack of reading ability. These comments tend to arouse the sceptic in me.
Very often it turns out they mean they lose large groups when they feel they
shouldn't. Poor strategy and bad feeling for shape are just as often the
cause of their defeats, as lack of ability at the analysis of given positions.
There is not much that has been said about Go that is wiser than the comment
that you should steer the game into positions you can read out.

However, most of us can do with practice in the area of problem solving.
Here is a collection of capturing races, of the simplest sort (three liberties
left on the chain, so that these are all in a sense loose ladders – you have on
average to fill a liberty each turn). Answers at the end of the chapter. Black
to play in each case. To add interest, *Black can win the race in exactly five
out of the six examples.* Capturing races in general haven't been given a
systematic treatment; have a look at *The Second Book of Go* (Kiseido, new
edition).

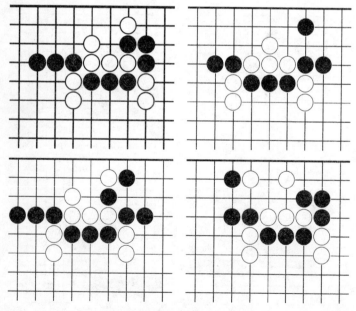

1,2,3,4. Capturing race problems – Black to play.

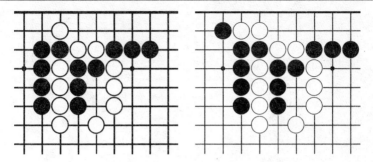

5,6. Final pair of capturing race problems – Black to play.

12.5 Solutions

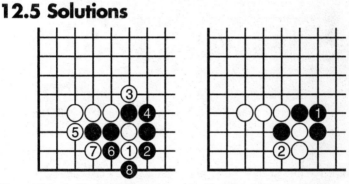

From 12.3. **1. (Left)** White gets good value by adding one stone.
2. (Right) Black should connect at 1 before anything else.

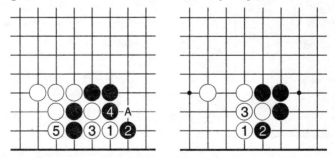

3. (Left) White should leave a cutting point at A, by playing the diagonal move at 1 here. **4. (Right)** White makes a sound shape with 1.

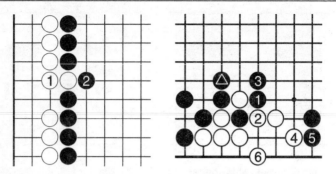

5. (Left) White 1 means Black 2 isn't *atari*. **6. (Right)** Black should just play the marked stone, to allow 1 later to take away an eye.

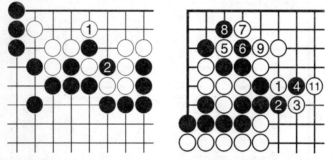

7. (Right) White gives up one stone and can play elsewhere. **8. (Left)** White holds the *atari* plays in the corner in reserve. For example, in this case, (Black 10 at 5) Black's cut at 4 is a failure.

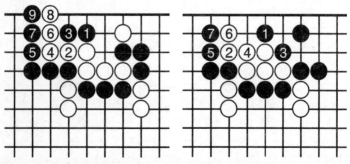

From 12.4. **1. (Left)** Black wins with the nose play at 1.
2. (Right) Black wins in a similar way.

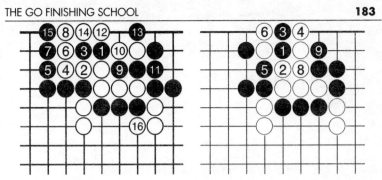

3. (Left) This is the case in which Black fails. White has just enough time to win the fight. **4. (Right)** Black 7 at 1. Black wins.

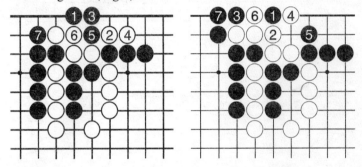

5,6. Black wins here by clever placements on the first line.

The priest's
      wife
         has
           to
           ring
           the
            bell
             because
               the
                  game is still going on.
(My very loose translation of a *senryu* about Go.)

13 | A CLASSIC MATCH

13.1 Professional and amateur

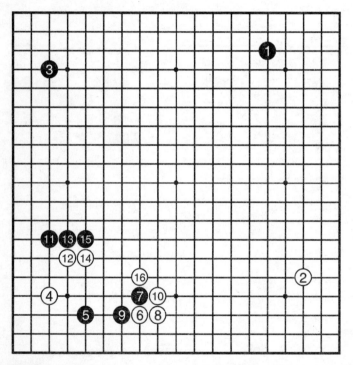

(1–16) This chapter is devoted to a game from 1851. Sekiyama Sendaiu, who took Black, was one of the greatest amateur players of all time. His opponent, Kuwahara Shusaku of the Honinbo house, enjoyed unrivalled success in the 'castle Go' series of matches played before the *shōgun*. His style is still considered to be a model to study for aspiring players.

13.2 A lively start

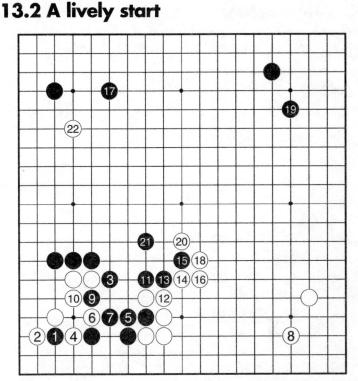

(1–22) The opening plays of the game make for a lively development, with both players using the 5–3 point. The corner opening on the last this and the previous page resolves itself as a trade of a Black wall on the left side for a White wall on the lower side. A *ko* position remains, but is never seriously contested as the game goes on. Things to notice here:

- ■ The exchange of 11 and 12 is similar to the solution to problem 4 on p.179.

- ■ Black's two enclosures at the top are unorthodox, oriented towards building influence.

- ■ The play at 18 is a good example of occupation of a focal point, an idea introduced on p.172.

- ■ Black 21 avoids making an empty triangle.

This game was number 19 out of a 20 game challenge match. It was played over two days. Shusaku was 6 *dan* at the time.

13.3 Tidy defence

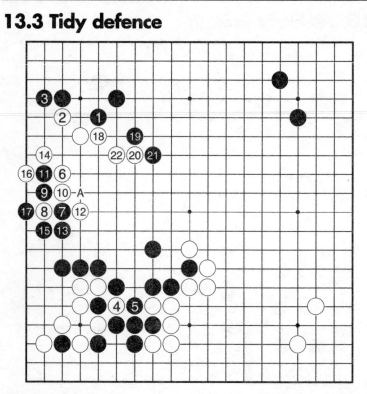

(1–22) White had invaded the left side at the end of the previous diagram.
White comes under some pressure here, but sacrifices a stone with 8 and
builds a defensible position. At the end of the sequence, White is left with
a serious cutting point at A. If Black cuts there now, White will have to
give up the stone 12. Black will not do this soon – it would amount to
'making territory next to thickness' (p.171), though you could say the Black
stones aren't genuine 100 per cent thickness, just close to it on the spectrum
of influence from Chapter 11. White is quick to remind Black of a cutting
point by taking the *ko* with 4.

This game illustrates also the idea that in Go each player may have to attack
and defend in turn. Good defence can be recognized by a tidy approach to
developing eye shape or running away, and an effort to leave weaknesses in
the attacker's formation for later. You can see the latter point when the
players return to this part of the board in 40 moves' time.

13.4 All-out fighting

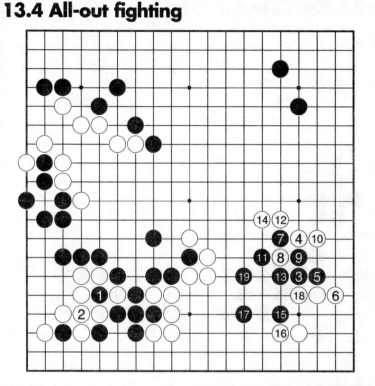

(1–19) Black comes in deeply to reduce White's area on the lower side. White reacts, not by defending territory here, but with a strategy of keeping Black's group weak. In due course this will lead to fighting which engulfs most of the rest of the board. Once more it can be said that Go is an indirect game. White deals with the Black framework stretching across the top of the board, but not by direct invasion. You should be able to see that the ladder with 11 is good for Black. However, Black cannot make two eyes in the restricted area in the lower right, as White proceeds to prove.

Shusaku was born in 1829, in the west of Honshu, the main island of Japan. He was awarded his professional diploma at age 10, by the head of the Honinbo house. He was aged 22 at the time of this match, reaching the peak of his powers very young for a Go player. Thirty-five is normally considered the prime age. His opponent Sekiyama was a *samurai* by birth, and 67 years old.

13.5 The fight spreads

(1–26) With 1 and 3 White destroys Black's eye shape, so Black heads for the centre. White has his own worries in this fight. The group on the lower side seems to be floating by the end of the sequence given, while White's group in the upper left appears to have been weakened too. Both these effects result from Black's determined play from 12 on in the centre. The peeping exchange of 10 for 11 makes White's right side look fragile also.

The circumstances of the match were unusual. The games were played every day for three weeks in the month of June. Sekiyama took Black in each game and won seven out of 20. This would be a respectable result for one of today's lower ranked professionals playing a top titleholder, let alone an amateur taking on one of the all time great players. Such was the intensity of interest in Go in *samurai* circles in the long peace of the Edo period in Japan. More about those times in 14.2.

13.6 White handles the situation

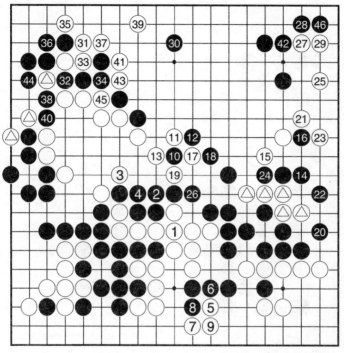

(1–46) Now White gets a grip on the game, and sets up the victory. He settles the lower side by connecting with 5, 7 and 9. Then he strengthens the centre with 11 and 13. Next Shusaku proceeds to sacrifice the five marked stones on the right side in return for a way into the top right corner with 23 and 27. Decisively, White makes the most of Black's residual weakness in the top left from 31 onwards, sacrificing a further three marked stones.

A balance sheet up to 44 would show that White has not conceded much in terms of territory, while handling all the difficulties. And the situation on the top side now favours an invasion backed by thickness on the left, a good example for 11.6. Altogether this way of playing exemplifies the Japanese term *sabaki*, skilful handling.

13.7 The invasion comes at last

(1–19) White 1, here, was play 152 in the game. It finally answers the question of how White will deal with the framework Black built on the top side with his first two plays of the game. It is also a fine example for 11.6, on invasions backed up by thickness. Appearances to the contrary, perhaps, the upper left is now 'thick' for White.

Black reacts, not with passive defence, but by threatening the White group in the top right. At the end of the figure there is still a *ko* fight to be played out, to settle whether it has two eyes. But while White is weaving a web in the centre with 9, 11 and 17, Black must walk a tightrope in trying to save both sides. After 16, Black has secured the top right corner.

Note that the marked Black stones are not important at present. In the sense explained on p.44, they are not cutting stones (White has another capture). At this stage a rough count reveals that White will win easily if Black 8 is captured. However, that is unlikely – White still has a *ko* to fight.

13.8 Resolutions

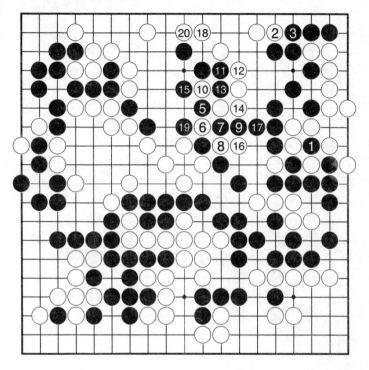

(1–20) White 4 retakes *ko* below 1.

The *ko* on the right side is one for which White has a local threat, at 2. After that Black concentrates on finding a way out in the centre. The final big fight of the game comes to a peaceful conclusion as White heads for the edge with 18, and Black allows him to connect out.

Shusaku died in 1862, of cholera, at the age of 33. Upheavals in Japan, political and social, in the next few decades led to a relative decline of Go from a peak of excellence in the first half of the nineteenth century. One can compare the careers of Shusaku, and of the American chess player Paul Morphy who dominated chess in the late 1850s just as Shusaku dominated the 'castle' Go. Go derived enormous advantages from state support: a guaranteed career for top players, constant competition, and an apprenticeship system.

13.9 The endgame

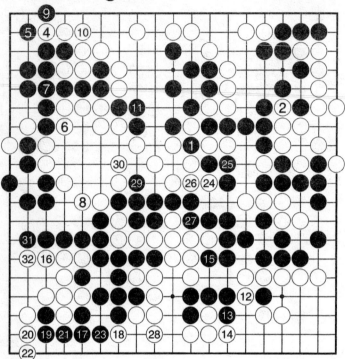

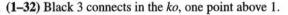

(1–32) Black 3 connects in the *ko*, one point above 1.

After White makes sure of the top right group, and Black closes down the *ko* in the upper centre, White concentrates on tidying up the top left. White 4 is important because this point might shortly become *sente* for both. White 8 finally covers the cutting point first mentioned in 13.3. When White makes this 10 point patch of territory in the centre it must have been clear to both players that White had won, and the only question was the margin.

There is a story attached to this match. This game was the penultimate nineteenth; the final twentieth game was won by Sekiyama by one point. It is said that Shusaku threw the game, losing deliberately. This casts a chink of light onto the character of the man. His life was documented in a book, and he became a posthumous celebrity. For many years the first task given to an *insei* (student professional) was to play through Shusaku's games.

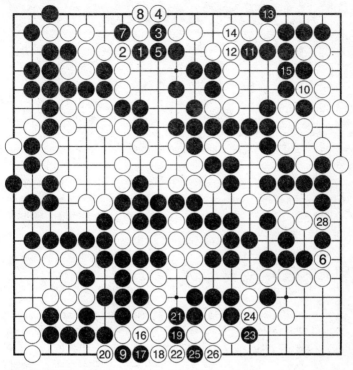

(1–28) Black 27 at 9.

There are some technically interesting points about the endgame plays in this diagram. Black sacrifices stones such as 7 and 23, in the knowledge they will be captured, but that White will make extra moves inside to do so.

Black resigned on seeing White 28. There is no problem for Black to capture this White chain, but Black in turn will be forced to play some extra moves inside his territory, to take off the White stones. Black took the opportunity of resignation at a good moment – a matter of dignity. For a Go player, knowing when and how to bow out of a lost game is part of the art of playing.

A rough count of the game suggests that Black would have lost by half a dozen points. You might care to play out the game from the position reached. The biggest plays now left are worth about three points.

14 | MORE ABOUT GO

This chapter concentrates on topics of general interest to do with Go. It includes references to the many Go web sites to be found on the World Wide Web. To get an instant idea of the range of the Internet coverage consult Ken Warkentyne's outstanding links page at **http://nngs.cosmic.org/hmkw/golinks.html**. NB We give names in formal book references in *Western order*, personal+family; otherwise Oriental names are family+personal.

14.1 Origins

It is generally accepted that the origins of Go lie in China, or possibly in neighbouring parts of Central Asia. It is also often assumed that the equipment of a grid and pebbles preceded the game we know – quite possibly employed for divination. The exact age of Go is another matter. Games expert David Pritchard has cast doubt on the often-quoted figure of 4,000 years for the game, which would put its origin at 2000 BCE, very early in Chinese recorded history. On the other hand there is evidence in Confucian texts around 500 BCE for a game some scholars identify with Go. It is much safer to say that Go is between 2,500 and 3,000 years old, but not to insist on a figure. John Fairbairn discusses the literary and archaeological evidence in depth on his web site. His conclusion is much the same.

Surviving Go literature from China is about 1,000 years old (problems exist over 600 years old), but equipment from Japan predates it by several hundred years. Some early game records are known, but in this area pious frauds are hard to eliminate.

Go played a part in the traditional picture of the Chinese scholar-gentleman. The complete mandarin would number among his accomplishments poetry, calligraphy, music and Go. It is interesting to see this as a definition of balance, in the personality of an intellectual. It seems that by the Song period the literary side was stressed almost to the exclusion of other traditions, such as military theory. If so, Go can be regarded as a kind of refined residual of that aspect of the culture. See Chapter 15 of Gernet's book cited below.

http://www.harrowgo.demon.co.uk

The above is the web site of John Fairbairn, Go author, translator and historian. It contains, besides history, much of interest to the Go player, for example, top level games on 9x9 boards.

Books: Joseph Needham's *Science and Civilisation in China* (CUP) discusses divination, boards used for it, and connections with games, as part of its survey of pre-scientific ideas. Jacques Gernet's *History of Civilisation in China* is published in English translation, by CUP.

14.2 Go under the Tokugawa shogunate

Go arrived in Japan at the same time as much else in Chinese culture, in the centuries from 600 CE onwards, brought on the tide of Buddhist influence. An association with particular Buddhist sects continued. Earlier it had spread to the kingdoms of the Korean peninsula.

The Japanese view of their own Go tradition is very much conditioned by its development during the long period (1603–1867) of the Tokugawa *shōguns*. In the years after the unification by Tokugawa Ieyasu, who founded a dynasty of *shōguns* wielding the real power in the land, Japan was effectively closed to most external influence. The period is also called after Edo, the old name for Tokyo.

The state supported Go from 1612 by means of four main 'houses' or academies, the Hayashi, Honinbo, Inoue and Yasui. Go was cultivated as a Japanese tradition with teachers and disciples, and the assumption of the total devotion of the adept to its mastery, little explicit attention being paid to Chinese origins (and contact cut off, though books travelled). The appearance of verses about Go in the form of *senryu*, metrically the same as *haiku* but satirical, mocking or low in content, confirms that Go was at the same time part of everyday life. It would be wrong, according to John Fairbairn, to assume that Japanese players were at all times during these centuries superior to all others. In particular, during the eighteenth century, the level in Japan sagged somewhat, while there were outstanding players in China. But this period has shaped the subsequent history of Go in many important ways:

- The level required to be a top player rose sharply, probably to at least two grades beyond today's strong amateurs (5 *dans*).

- A system of ranks from 1 *dan* to 9 *dan* was imposed, comparable as a hierarchy to the court ranks, which went back to China and Confucian ideas of respect and orderliness.

- Exhibition games ('castle Go', played in the presence of the *shōgun* or his representative) and extended matches between representatives of the four houses provided competition of high seriousness.

- The top grade, *Meijin* ('expert'), or 9 *dan*, was awarded to the outstanding player in a generation. This appointment, a 'Go Laureate', was the subject of much intrigue.

The game changed too. Japanese players started with the board clear, where the Chinese traditionally began with corner 4–4 stones in place. New corner openings (*joseki*) were studied in depth, especially the pincer openings for the 3–4 point. Meijin Dosaku (1645–1702), fourth head of the Honinbo house and 'canonised' as *kisei*, Go sage or saint, brought in new theoretical concepts. *Korigatachi* (overconcentration) and *amarigatachi* (broken shape caused by over-the-top attack) began to be driven from top level play. *Katachi* (good shape) and *tesuji* (key point plays) became a teachable foundation for Go. The game was slowed down, with emphasis on the *honte* (proper move), and less fear of the opponent's frameworks.

http://www.honinbo.freeserve.co.uk/

The above is a very full site, with game records, based on an extended series of articles by Andrew Grant in the *British Go Journal*, covering the whole period and more. See also John Fairbairn's site mentioned in 14.1.

Books: *Appreciating Famous Games* by Shuzo Ohira, *Invincible: The Games of Shusaku*, ed. John Power, both published by Kiseido.

14.3 Recent times

After the Meiji Restoration in 1868 the fortunes of Go in Japan took a turn for the worse, with the traditional houses losing their favoured position, in a period of westernization. A new organization, the Hoensha or 'Square-

Round Society', filled the gap. Go regained public attention through newspaper columns (seemingly adapted from the chess column in the London *Times*). The head of the Honinbo house, Shusai, played a prominent part in some high-profile matches in the early twentieth century, his 1926 clash with Karigane being posted on billboards as the game went on. He was awarded the *Meijin* title by acclaim of the other professionals – he would prove to be both the final Honinbo and the last of the traditional Meijins, though these titles survive in modern tournament Go. The founding of the Nihon Ki-in in 1924 brought order and state support once more to the Japanese Go world. Young stars emerged. Wu Qingyuan (b.1915), was a young prodigy from China, already of professional 5 *dan* strength in his early teens. He is better known by the Japanese reading Go Seigen of his name, which he adopted on becoming naturalized. He took on Meijin Shusai in a spectacular game in 1933, aged only 18. Wu lost narrowly, but his rival Kitani Minoru defeated Shusai in 1939 in an intense game played over many months. It was made the subject of Kawabata's novel *The Master of Go* (also called *Meijin*); see 14.6. Wu was the dominant figure in the period 1940–60, with a tremendous record in match play.

14.4 The professional scene

The post-war years in Japan saw Go at a height of popularity it may never regain there, though the spread of the game internationally now compensates, and there are hundreds of professional players. Newspapers set up titles to be fought over each year. First the Honinbo name that Shusai had left to the Nihon Ki-in was contested, with a challenger meeting the holder in a seven game match. Gradually a system of major titles evolved, now including Kisei and Meijin, with elaborate qualification systems and a matchplay culmination. Kisei is the top title for prestige and money (currently 32 million yen to the winner). Cho Chikun, Korean by birth but at the time of writing the most outstanding player in Japan, has won enough prize money to make him a yen billionaire.

From about 1970 onwards the international dimension has been increasingly important to Go, with the first credible world titles arriving at the end of the 1980s. In China there emerged Nie Weiping, a first undoubted 9 *dan*. Despite political difficulties in the aftermath of the Cultural Revolution, Go carrying a strong Confucian taint, the Zhongguo Qiyuan was set up to foster chess and *xiangqi* (Chinese chess) as well as *weiqi* (Go). Later Ma Xiaochun, and now the younger Chang Hao (b.1976), have had a major impact in the international tournaments of the past decade. The Chinese women players, including Rui Naiwei 9 *dan* who now lives in the USA, are the strongest in the world.

In South Korea the corresponding body is the Hanguk Kiwon, and the top players are Cho Hun-hyun and Seo Bong-soo of the older generation, Yoo Chang-hyuk and Lee Chang-ho. Lee (b.1975) turned professional at age 11 and started winning titles in his mid-teens. He has never stopped winning, and winning mysteriously, moving smoothly from the prodigy tag to the status of 'national treasure'. Most people would now rate him as the top player in the world. He hides uncharted depths behind a sphinx-like poker face.

http://www.nihonkiin.or.jp/index-e.htm

The above site is for the English-language pages of the Nihon Ki-in. From the home page you can find the Japanese pages (though your browser will need extra software to show them correctly).

http://www.nihonkiin.or.jp/kishi/htm/ki000174.htm

This web site is the home page of Michael Redmond 8 *dan*, the American from Santa Barbara who has gone further than any other Westerner in the professional Go world. Well, at least you can look at the photo! Other occidental pros are James Kerwin (1 *dan*) from Minnesota (change 174 in the URL to 271), Hans Pietsch (2 *dan,* change to 354) from Germany, and Catalin Taranu (3 *dan*, change to 347) from Romania.

14.5 Go and the New Age

Some of the appeal of Go in the West comes from its genuine relation to traditional oriental thought. Indeed it may be found to be a portal on the cultural level, while retaining naturally enough its quality as a highly, though not exclusively, rational activity. Go can be seen as coming from the same general background as the *I Ching*, of divination in a purely combinatorial style. What makes a major difference when playing Go is that the feel of the game is not combinatorial, but conceptual. Military theory, in China from Sun Zi onwards, or based on *The Five Rings* for the Japanese, both illuminates and may be illustrated by Go. 'Strengthen to the left if you want to attack on the right' isn't a paradox on the Go board but a commonplace theory. I'll just give some brief bullet points.

- Boorman's thesis, that Mao Zedong was influenced by Go, is probably overblown, since while Mao played Go he was also soaked in military theory and the *Romance of the Three Kingdoms*.
- Balance in Go. This is important in many forms such as third line/fourth line, but hard to define. See the Ing URL below.
- Indirection. Go is a game in which primary goals are often not realized, because the opponent has many resources. One only wins by playing both purposefully and flexibly.
- 'Feminine' quality. Western players seem very often to take the *yin-yang* balance of the game to be unimportant. They play to emphasize the hard edge of their intellectual approach.
- Go as it arrived in the West had two raw qualities: (1) it travelled as an incomplete formalization of traditional practice; (2) the aestheticization of violence behind it was alien, though not essentially different from Eiji Yoshikawa's popular *samurai* novel *Musashi*, or the *kung fu* movie. The West has probably changed more than Go in the mean time.
- *Grayfolded*, a layered compilation CD of Grateful Dead live performances of 'Dark Star', contains Jerry Garcia's thoughts on Go in the liner notes.

My own experience is that working over substantial tracts of the oriental literature teaches, above all, the distinction between literary and scientific approaches – the traditional anthologist of a poetic genre selects, where the Victorian entomologist collects and subclassifies.

http://home.sprynet.com/sprynet/vrmlpro/book.htm

A site about *EZ GO – Oriental Strategy in a Nutshell* (Ki Press), by Bruce and Sue Wilcox, ISBN 0-9652235-4-X. A very different introduction from this one, belonging in this section.

http://www.nbbj.com/GOECUL~3.htm

A Taiwanese page about balance.

Other books: *Go: An Asian Paradigm for Business Strategy* (Ishi) by Yasuyuki Miura; *The Protracted Game* (OUP) by Scott Boorman; *The Thirty Six Stratagems Applied to Go* (Yutopian) by Xiaochun Ma; and *Beauty and the Beast* (Yutopian) by Guosun Shen.

14.6 Go in literature and film

Go is mentioned in numerous places in classic novels from the East. *The Tale of Genji* by Shikibu Murasaki from the Heian period of Japan build Go into the plot of court life at points, though readers of the Waley translation were deprived of some of the references, which can be found in the more literal Seidensticker translation. *The Story of the Stone* by Cao Xueqin from China, features Go games as part of the life of the privileged.

Kawabata Yasunari, who won the Nobel Prize for Literature in 1968, was a keen amateur Go player. His book *The Master of Go* (Vintage International), already mentioned in 14.3, is a lightly fictionalized account of the retirement match of Honinbo Shusai. Kawabata was the *Mainichi Shinbun* reporter at the game, writing 64 columns about it. (See **http://www.cwi.nl/~jansteen/ go/stories/8.html** for more background.) It has been praised as the best book ever written about games and games-players. The match, a single game played over many sessions as Shusai's health failed, and ending in his narrow defeat, is set in the time of the 'China Emergency' before Pearl Harbor. The novel is profoundly elegiac in tone, as the author renders his feelings about the old Japan slipping away alongside the protracted play of the game. Kawabata's *Japan, The Beautiful and Myself*, based on his Nobel acceptance speech, can stand as his generation's tribute to the culture of their forebears, in which Go is included without the slightest inconsistency.

Western authors of science fiction allude to Go, often without much apparent understanding. *Shibumi* by Trevanian has a thriller plot and a hero who is represented as a Go player.

http://www.cam.ac.uk/CambUniv/Societies/cugos/tesuji/chikamat.htm

This is a page of mine about a drama of Chikamatsu involving Go, with more Immortals (cf. p. 71). The text is from a translation by Donald Keene.

Films

Go is comparatively rare in films seen in the West. The original *Godzilla* (1954) is said to feature a scene with sailors peacefully playing Go on the deck of a ship, before the mutant monster rises from the deep. Kurosawa's *Sanjuro* (1962), the light-hearted sequel to *Yojimbo* (which was remade as *A Fistful of Dollars*), has a scene with a *goban*, the traditional Japanese board that stands on the floor. Mifune Toshiro as the 'Samurai-with-No-Name' has to whip into vengeful shape an unpromising crowd of soft retainers of a *daimyo* (lord). He harangues them while squatting on the *goban*, demonstrating his lack of culture. *The Fate of Lee Khan*, by King Hu, has a scene with the hated Mongol guards playing Go (about 17 *kyu*, I'd say, unless the acting was superb). And Go features in the successful independent film *Pi* (1998), in a rather stereotypical way as an interest of the mathematician central character.

14.7 Computer Go

The business of trying to program a computer to play Go has attracted increasing interest. It has been realized that techniques used for other games of skill, and increasing speed in the hardware, are not going to produce a program of amateur *dan* level in the near future. The available Go software is useful to provide opposition to those learning the game, up to about 10 *kyu* (weak club player); but performs badly against strong amateurs, even with a large handicap. A large bet offered by Ing Chang-ki, a Taiwanese businessman, would have made a dollar millionaire of any programmer able to make a machine defeat a professional Go player. But Mr Ing died in 1997 without his money looking in any danger.

There are many aspects to the question, starting with simple matters of formalizing the rules of play, and leading onto highly speculative matters in artificial intelligence.

Counting liberties

A useful place to start is to ask how the computer can count liberties on a chain. Without that capacity machines cannot play legally or 'see' captures. What is required is that the computer keeps lists of the chains of Black and White stones, and of their liberties. Each time a stone is played these lists must be updated. This involves the following:

- Creating a new chain if the stone is played in an isolated position.
- Amalgamating two or more chains if the stone is played as a solid connection between chains.
- Removing one or more chains if the stone played is a capture.
- Finally making consequent changes to the liberties on the new list of chains.

These operations can be reduced to a routine, and the most complicated game positions can therefore be analysed into chains and liberties. The point is that updating every turn is a reliable if dull way of doing this.

Machines gladly perform such tasks, the precise details not being an issue for us. The human approach is likely to be very different and certainly less systematic. If despite reading Chapter 3 you feel there is something a little fuzzy about the rules relating to capture, playing through part of a game with the steps just outlined in mind may help to clarify them.

Counting eyes

Assuming some further work to ensure that the computer respects the *ko* and suicide rules, one can envisage a basic program: one that plays legal Go. Looking for targets (3.2) is easy with a list of chains and liberties. But what about the step up to the systematic use of techniques of attack and defence of eyes (Chapter 5)?

The experience of Dave Dyer with a program using the patterns from 5.6 shows up the strengths and limitations of machines. The number of unsettled shapes (5.7) is limited. Symmetries were dealt with tacitly in Chapter 5, as seems sensible for humans. When they were restored, variations with occupants listed, and defects affecting status noted, the database of fundamental patterns had swelled to around 500,000. A computer having all this information available by 'look-up' would in principle determine the status of groups with 100 per cent success. Human players with a little experience might be wrong 10 per cent of the time (*dan* players ought not to make any mistakes). But the scale of the effort required to reduce even this small corner of 'life and death' to the mechanical application of pattern-matching indicates the difficulties – humans are simply much better at using this kind of information in compressed form.

Counting on territory

The end of the game presents a problem, computationally speaking. One reason for pessimism about Go programs and their future development is that the middlegame is even worse

Every experienced player knows that you must watch carefully at the end of the game for break-in and live-inside disasters, commonly known as swindles. Right at the end of the game, before passing, one has to assess each territory on the board, to see whether the filling-in of some outside liberty, or the appearance of some cutting point, has changed its status from impregnable to vulnerable.

Certainly any problem out of a broad range on the status of a group, of deciding whether it is dead or unsettled, may appear at this stage. Specialized programs, such as Thomas Wolf's *GoTools*, can tackle such questions, though at the cost of a great deal of computation in some cases. But one aspect of its operation should be noticed: the situation must be given some definite boundary conditions, solid outside walls that delimit the area of search.

Problems of this kind occur much earlier in the game, but without the comfort of aids to posing the question exactly. Invasions are part of the give-and-take of the middlegame. 'Is there an invasion of that enemy territory, and if so, how much trouble do I stir up on the rest of the board if I go through with it?' This is a commonplace query for a player, who may answer it in some fashion that would be hard for any program to match. You certainly can't count on any territory of your own until you put yourself in the opponent's shoes, and deal with the problem the other way round also.

http://www.reiss.demon.co.uk/webgo/compgo.htm

Mick Reiss on computer Go. Mick is one of the leading Go programmers (*Go++*, marketed as *Go Professional*). His page has many links to others dealing with the issues in Go programming.

http://andromeda.com/people/ddyer/go-program.html

This page by Dave Dyer is a reference for the work mentioned in the text.

http://www.britgo.demon.co.uk/reviews/

This page of software reviews is updated regularly.

http://alpha.qmw.ac.uk/~ugah006/gotools/index.html

Thomas Wolf's *GoTools* is an MS-DOS program for solving life and death problems, mentioned above.

Commercial software

There are a number of programs of similar strength (*Go Professional, Handtalk, Many Faces of Go* being the leading ones) that are useful opponents for beginners. They rate as weak club player level (8 *kyu*).

Freeware, shareware, downloads

For a large range of downloadable Go software (freeware and shareware), look at **http://www.britgo.demon.co.uk/gopcres/gopcres1.html**. Highly recommended is the 9x9 version *igowin* of *Many Faces of Go*.

14.8 Algebraic notation and file formats

The pioneer players in the West found difficulty with Go diagrams. They were up against crowded woodcuts with the numerals in Chinese notation. As the years went by the perceived requirement for an algebraic system of notation in Go books receded; but it is clearly necessary for computer Go.

The earlier of the two main systems used dates back to Oskar Korschelt, who wrote on Go over a century ago. It uses natural coordinates to identify points in the style C4 for the point (3,4) three along and four up from the bottom left-hand corner. There is however a wrinkle: Korschelt being German left I out of the alphabet, so that the 10–10 point at the centre of the board is called K10, and the top right corner T19.

The file format based on this system uses the suffix or file extension of type **filename.go**. It is variously called Ishi or Standard.

The other candidate notation is called SGF, and derives from a general project in computer games programming. The form of the notation is [cd] for the point 3 along and 4 down from the *top* left corner of the board. The 10–10 point is therefore [jj] and the top right corner [sa].

The SGF file format uses a suffix or file extension of type **filename.sgf**. The suffix **filename.mgt** indicates a closely related format.

While Ishi files can normally be read by humans with a little effort, SGF files normally cannot. This is because the game tree, i.e. a game with variations, is presented in different ways. The Ishi format is probably what you'd expect, while the SGF format is designed for easy machine parsing.

Game files

The major reason for including this section is to explain how to obtain and read game files on a computer. Free PC programs to read the files, such as *Yago*, and shareware programs such as *My Go Tutor*, may be downloaded from the BGA web site, at the same URL as in 14.7. John Fairbairn's site in 14.1 has information about the Gogod range of games on disk (in Ishi format and recently in SGF too).

http://www.cwi.nl/~jansteen/go/index.html

Jan van der Steen's pages are a strong candidate for the best WWW Go site. Thousands of games may be downloaded as SGF files, including recent top-level games. Much else too.

http://www.britgo.demon.co.uk/tech/ishispec.html
http://www.sbox.tu-graz.ac.at/home/h/hollosi/sgf/index.html

Web references for the Ishi and SGF formats. Of interest to programmers.

14.9 Grades and handicaps

Handicap Go was touched upon in 2.4. The conventional handicap placings are in the Appendix. Handicap games between players of different skills are for teaching. The stronger player should try to play well and the weaker player with good fighting spirit. Where these roles are reversed someone is missing the point. The correct handicap between two players can be determined by a series of a few games, for example under 'three game change' (add or remove one handicap stone when one player wins three times in a row). In a Go club self-consistent grading can be achieved.

Grades are a subject of abiding interest to players, in relative and absolute terms, and for reasons good and bad. The amateur *dan* grades are set at a level that demands some devotion to the game to attain – a pale copy perhaps of the depth of study behind the making of a professional, but a taste of single-mindedness. Three years to *shodan* (1 *dan*) is expected, even with some flair. Amateur 5 *dan* should represent 'strong amateur', able to face a professional with a three-stone handicap.

The traditional system of nine *dan* levels for professional players is set closer together. Theoretically from 1 *dan* to 9 *dan* the difference is three stones. These days the total spread is more like two stones. Amateur *dan* grades form a separate system. Professional level is about 8 *dan* on the amateur scale. It is usually considered that top professionals are about 2 stones from perfect play. There is no Elo-style rating system, and *dan* grades are supposed to be for life. Grade inflation is very commonly seen at the amateur levels, and grades are not consistent internationally. The Korean system (with *gup* for *kyu*) is the most stringent, followed by the Chinese, European, American, then Japanese.

14.10 Books, magazines and equipment

The number of books on Go written in English is not small: there are perhaps 50 worth reading, and more are published each year. The oriental literature is huge. Problem books are easy to study in any language, using the diagrams and a few words. It has become much simpler to find Go books, for example, from the major online bookshops; search by author, title, or publisher of one book and you'll come across others. A very full English bibliography is at **http://math.stanford.edu/~carlton/go/** (links for French, Italian).

Other introductions

Other books starting from the beginning include *Go for Beginners* (Pantheon) by Kaoru Iwamoto; *Go: A Complete Introduction* (Kiseido) by Chikun Cho; *Learn to Play Go* (Good Move Press) by Janice Kim, which has turned into a series. The four volumes of *Graded Go Problems for Beginners* (Kiseido) by Yoshinori Kano start with very elementary problems in Volume 1; Volume 2 would usefully accompany the early chapters of this book. *The Go Pack* (Carlton) by Matthew Macfadyen includes a set.

General books

The following books follow this one, in seeking to give a broad coverage. They are in rough order of difficulty.
The Second Book of Go (Kiseido) by Richard Bozulich; *Master Go in Ten Days* (Yutopian) by Xu Xiang and Jin Jiang Zheng; *Basic Techniques of Go* (Kiseido) by Isamu Haruyama and Yoshiaki Nagahara; *Lessons in the Fundamentals of Go* (Kiseido) by Toshiro Kageyama; *Strategic Concepts of Go* (Kiseido) by Yoshiaki Nagahara. Two classics, *Go Proverbs Illustrated* by Kensaku Segoe, and *Vital Points of Go* by Kaku Takagawa, published by the Nihon Ki-in, are out of print.

Topics

Here the author to look for is James Davies, in titles published by Kiseido. All the Davies books, including those written in collaboration with professionals, are well organized and readable. His *Life and Death* and *Tesuji* are among the first books to buy. The *Get Strong* series of problem books by Kiseido has built up into a substantial library. Among the Yutopian books *Tesuji and Anti-Suji of Go* by Eio Sakata is one of the best.

Magazines

The international English-language magazine *Go World* (Kiseido) is quarterly and covers the top professional games, with commentary. National associations produce their own magazines.

Equipment

Go equipment is sold by the specialist suppliers who stock Go books. You can find it in games shops too. Boards and stones of good quality, and turned wooden bowls, can be very attractive; but also expensive. Glass stones and wooden boards come in various thicknesses. If you feel tempted to make a board of your own, you should note that boards are not square but rectangular, being about 8 per cent longer than broad to compensate for foreshortening.

http://www.britgo.demon.co.uk/bgabooks/bgaprices.html

BGA Books, 10 Vine Acre, Monmouth, Gwent NP5 3HW, UK. Tel. +44 (0)1600 712934 . Email **bgabooks@btinternet.com**. Supplies a full range of books by mail order, and equipment. The web page links to a page of other suppliers.

http://www.labnet.or.jp/~kiseido/, http://www.yutopian.com

Kiseido and Yutopian, the major Go publishers (also suppliers). Email **kiseido@crl.com** (Kiseido USA), **gostuff@webwind.com** (Yutopian).

http://www.xs4all.nl/~paard/, email **paard@xs4all.nl**

Schaak en Gowinkel 'het Paard' is a major supplier in Amsterdam.

14.11 Useful addresses

British Go Association: Web site **http://www.britgo.demon.co.uk**, email **bga@britgo.demon.co.uk**. Postal address The Hollies, Wollerton, Market Drayton, Shropshire TF9 3LY, UK. Tel. +44 (0)1630 685292. Join the BGA for the quarterly *British Go Journal*, bi-monthly newsletter, tournament information and discounts. The web site lists Go clubs in Britain.

American Go Association: **http://www.usgo.org** , email **aga@usgo.org**. Postal address: PO 397 Old Chelsea Station, New York NY 10113.

Australian Go Association: **http://www.adfa.oz.au/~dle/**, email **Neville.Smythe@anu.edu.au**. Postal address: GPO Box 65, Canberra ACT, Australia 2601.

Canadian Go Association: **http://www.uwinnipeg.ca/~erbach/cga**, email **erbach@io.uwinnipeg.ca**. Postal address: 71 Brixford Crescent Winnipeg Manitoba R2N 1E1.

European Go Federation: **http://kate.kttl.helsinki.fi/egf**. *European Go Cultural Centre*: **http://www.xs4all.nl/~egcc/index.html**, email **egcc@xs4all.nl**. Postal address: Schokland 14 1181 HV Amstelveen, Netherlands.

Nederlandse Go Bond: **http://www.gobond.nl/**. Contact via the EGCC.

Fédération Française de Go: **http://bat710.univ-lyon1.fr/~ffg/**, email **drkropp@magic.fr**. Postal address: BP95 75262 Paris cedex 06.

Deutscher Go Bund: **http://www.zpr.uni-koeln.de/~gawron/dgob**, email **dgob@zpr.uni-koeln.de**. Postal address: Postfach 60 54 54 22249 Hamburg.

New Zealand: Auckland Go Club, email **mtaler@ait.ac.nz**.

South African Go Association: **http://users.iafrica.com/h/hu/hunt/saga**. Postal address: PO Box 561 Parklands Johannesburg 2121. Tel. +27 11 678 2798.

All other countries: Consult the links pages **http://www.usgo.org/world/orgs.html** and **http://www.xs4all.nl/~egcc/egf/europe.html**. Systematic email addresses and URLs in Europe follow the patterns **italy@european-go.org** and **http://italy.european-go.org** based on country names in English.

14.12 Go servers, other Internet resources

It has become easy to play Go online. A full list of Go servers may be found at **http://www.britgo.demon.co.uk/gopcres/play.html#server**. The Internet Go Server (IGS), at **http://igs.joyjoy.net**, is the largest Go server, and is English-language. It is based on Telnet, as is the smaller NNGS (Telnet to **nngs.cosmic.org**). To use these servers you will have to download a client program. Consult the URL given for more information. Yahoo! Go, to be found at **http://games.yahoo.com**, is currently less suitable for serious games, but is Java-based and can be used easily with browser only.

There are several ways to play Go by email. One is to email **jjw6@psu.edu** to be put onto a monthly list. There is a newsgroup **rec.games.go**. Its FAQ is posted: **ftp://rtfm.mit.edu/pub/faqs/games/go-faq**.

APPENDIX: RULES OF GO

The subject of the rules of Go is a broad one, in principle stretching from comical queries such as 'Is there a rule against tracing a ladder out on the board with your finger?' (no, but this is considered *gauche*, at the very least), to arcane trivia such as 'What rules are used in Sikkim?' (the Tibetan kind, though that may leave you no wiser). Those who are interested in *instructions on how to play* should be aware that much discussion about rule sets is about *precise definition of Go*. The truth of the matter is that there are a number of very closely related variants, making the primitive concept of Go into a playable game, such that your skill at one transfers to the others at a level of well over 99 per cent. No set of rules that is considered to define Go requires an adjustment from the player anything like as serious as the transfer from rubber bridge to duplicate bridge, for example.

The rules used in this book are the Japanese rules, those operated by the Nihon Ki-in. We mentioned area counting in 8.11, but otherwise no concession has been made to other rule sets. Here are the simplest variants to describe:

- ■ **Size of board:** 19x19 is the standard. 17x17 was used in historical times. 21x21 is the next experiment to try, but the game would become long.

- ■ **Initial position.** Beginning with an empty board is now the international standard. But the traditional Chinese start was D4 and Q16 for one player, D16 and Q4 for the other. The Korean equivalent was more elaborate yet: D4, G4, N4, D10, K10, Q10, G16, N16, Q16 for Black, K4, Q4, D7, Q7, D13, Q13, D16, K16 for White. (Ishi notation – see 14.8.)

- ■ **Handicap placings.** For the record here's the Japanese system. Two stones: D4 and Q16; for three stones, the only asymmetric case, add D16 as White looks at the board (the Chinese often use K10 instead); four stones add Q4; five stones add K10. For six stones remove K10 and add D10 and Q10; seven stones replace K10; eight stones remove K10 and add K4 and K16;

and nine stones replace K10. So in old China 3–4 openings were for handicap games!

■ *Komi.* White is compensated for starting second in even games, by the award of five and a half points, in almost all professional tournaments in Japan, preventing draws. Before about 1950 most games were played without *komi*, giving Black a considerable advantage. *Komi* has increased, from four and a half points as a norm; and may be increased again in future, since many players feel that modern opening research has given Black an edge. Games with large *komi*, calculated at a rate around 10 points for a stone, are interesting as a change from handicaps in the form of stones.

Etiquette

As Black start in the top right corner (at R16 if you play a 3–4 point). As White don't play in your opponent's bottom right corner if the first play was symmetrical. The principle here is to allow your opponent the bottom right, closest to the bowl of a right-handed player. This explains the precise placing with a two- or three-stone handicap, too. There is no obligation to announce '*atari*'. This was the old Japanese etiquette, but it is no longer used. As far as this author is concerned, saying 'there doesn't seem to be much left now ...' and suchlike offends against etiquette, if you mean 'pass'.

Folk rules about imitation play

There is no prohibition on 'mirror Go', diagonal imitation of your opponent with respect to the centre of the board, either with White, or with Black having started at 10–10. See p.212 for a diagram. It seems to have been an old Chinese folk rule that this was banned. But with boards of an even size there is a problem, which is why they aren't used.

Free placement of handicaps, small board Go

It is common in China and Taiwan to allow handicap stones to be placed anywhere you choose. This system is also much used in small board Go. There is no accepted system for converting a grade difference into handicaps for the smaller boards. For a 13x13 game one stone for every three grades isn't too far off. Nor is there agreement on how *komi* should be set on the smaller boards.

The debatable topics

The Japanese rules use the very high-order concept of territory ('all invasions fail to live, no *ko*'). It has been shown that a very low-level but intensive use of the mathematical concept of transitive closure defines a workable rule set, together with area counting and a no repetition rule (the 'New Zealand' rules).

Rules barring all repetition of the state of the game are usually called *superko*. To apply a superko rule you have to define the state of the game with care. It must clearly involve the board position, and indicate whose turn it is. What else? It must note if the last play was a pass, so that two passes in succession can end the game. For the Japanese rules you should add the signed difference in the numbers of captives, adjusted by any *komi*, plus the information needed to identify a *ko* capture last turn. For a superko plus area counting system the state may appear to be just the board position, turn, pass and *komi*. You cannot tell from this which are the legal plays. You have also to store and check against all previous pairs (position, turn).

A superko rule forces the game to end (though not necessarily in either player's lifetime). Generally defining the end of the game causes trouble. The SST rules try to apply Go-playing intuitions in the hard cases; they are used in the Ing tournaments.

Variants that aren't really Go

The *Tibetan rules* forbid immediate recapture in a snapback, and immediate play on points cleared by capture. An interesting variant is *Do Not Pass Go*, suicide forbidden. The player who has no legal play loses. Since you can't pass, you end up filling in your own points. Leaving *seki* out of it, players will fill down to just two eyes in each group, and then one will have to fill an eye. That signals the end: the opponent will take and go on to win. This game is like area counting, plus a tax of two points on each live group. *Capture Go* has been mentioned in 2.2. *Go on a general graph* of nodes and edges is easy to define under New Zealand rules; it could for example be a toroidal or three-dimensional board. It would only attract a computer (and possibly computers would be closer in strength to humans on a sufficiently random graph). Go seems to be interesting because territory in the plane is just hard enough to make. A worthy new idea is Elwyn Berlekamp's *Environmental Go*: a stack of numbered cards sits by the board. You can play on the board or pick up a card to add to your final score.

Bestiary

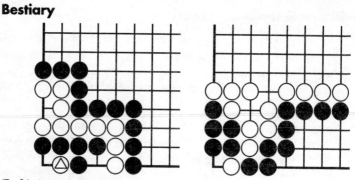

(Left) A capture within a *seki*, that can wait until the neutral points are filled. **(Right)** Neither player wants to capture. Traditionally 'three points for White, without capturing', a *seki* since the 1989 rules.

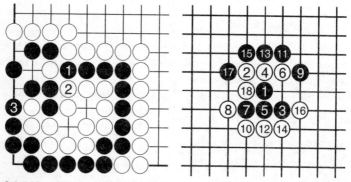

(Left) Life with an eye and false eyes, seen once a generation in pro play. Black would still be alive with the eye in the corner filled, as a 'double-headed dragon'. This example has been adapted from a game in the 1998 World Amateur Championship. **(Right)** One way to refute mirror Go.

http://www.inx.de/~jasiek/rules.html
Robert Jasiek on the rules.

http://www.eng.ox.ac.uk/people/Harry.Fearnley/go/bestiary/
various.html is Harry Fearnley's better bestiary.

http://www.cs.cmu.edu/~wjh/go/rules/SST.html
The SST rules, used in tournaments sponsored by the Ing Goe Foundation.

Books: *The Go Player's Almanac* (Kiseido) for the Japanese rules. *Mathematical Go* (AM Peters, Ishi) by Elwyn Berlekamp and David Wolfe.

GLOSSARY

Names for Go

The correct Japanese name for Go is *igo* (pronounced 'ee-goh'). The Chinese name is *weiqi* (pronounced 'way-chee', or 'why-kee'). The Korean word is *baduk* (pronounced 'bah-dook'). Goe is a spelling used by the Ing Foundation. If you are looking on the Internet, any one of these words is better for a search engine to chew on than 'Go', since go is a very common word in English.

Basic Go vocabulary

The working vocabulary drawn from Japanese in this book has deliberately been kept small, as befits a game that is becoming internationalized. The only words used freely are these:

- ■ *Atari* means to threaten, by filling a penultimate liberty.
- ■ *Dan* refers to the advanced grades held by expert amateurs, and professionals.
- ■ *Gote* ('goh-tay') means 'losing the initiative'.
- ■ *Ko* is a potentially repeating situation, that requires a rule.
- ■ *Komi* are the points given to White in an even game to compensate for playing second.
- ■ *Kyu* grades are the initial series of grades, before *dan* levels.
- ■ *Seki* is a local stalemate, persisting until the end of the game.
- ■ *Sente* ('sen-tay') means 'retaining the initiative'.

Please consult the Index for the first use of these and other terms. For reading other books: *chuban* is middlegame, *dame* is neutral point or liberty, *fuseki* is full board opening, *geta* is net, *hoshi* is a 4–4 or other star point, *ikken tobi* is one-point jump, *jigo* is a draw, *joseki* is corner opening, *kakari* is approach move, *keima* is knight's move, *komoku* is a 3–4 point, *kosumi* is a diagonal play, *moyo* is framework, *nirensei* is 'two stars' and *sanrensei* 'three stars', *semeai* is capturing race, *shibori* is squeeze, *shicho* is ladder, *shimari* is enclosure, *tsuke* is contact play, *watari* is bridging under, and *yose* is endgame.

INDEX